Feb 18, 2022

Feb 18, 2022

# The Ruby Chalice Visitations

# The Maha Chohan Speaks on
## The Ruby Chalice Visitations of the God Qualities

By
Monroe Julius Shearer
Carolyn Louise Shearer

The Ruby Chalice Visitations of the God Qualities
   Published by
Acropolis Sophia Books & Works®
   an Imprint of
The Temple of The Presence®
P.O. Box 17839
Tucson, Arizona 85731

www.TempleofThePresence.org

Text and Illustrations Copyright © 1996, 2005, 2006, 2021
by The Temple of The Presence, Inc.

All rights reserved.
No part of this book may be reproduced in any form or
by any means whatsoever without prior written permission,
except in the case of brief quotations embodied in articles
and reviews.

For information, write
   Acropolis Sophia Books & Works®
   P.O. Box 17839, Tucson, Arizona 85731

Printed in the United States of America
First Printing, 2021
Library of Congress Number: 2021920445
ISBN 978-1-7337302-8-0

Dictations presented in this book have been
prepared by the presiding Master for release
in written form for our present use and for
posterity.

# Table of Contents

| | |
|---|---|
| In The Beginning & Now by The Maha Chohan | 3 |
| A New Era and A New Dispensation by El Morya | 17 |
| My Ruby Chalice Visitations | 23 |
| Love | 29 |
| Harmony | 35 |
| Peace | 43 |
| Purity | 49 |
| Happiness I | 59 |
| Happiness II | 67 |
| Faith I | 73 |
| Faith II | 79 |
| Hope | 85 |
| Charity | 93 |
| Patience | 99 |
| Poise | 107 |
| Humility | 115 |
| Courage | 123 |
| Strength | 135 |
| Fearlessness | 143 |
| Fire | 153 |
| An Initiation in the Fire of the Ruby Chalice by Lord Maitreya | 163 |
| Invocation of The God Qualities | 171 |
| Calls for the Release of the Holy Spirit | 172 |
| Violet Fire Decree | 173 |

*The Maha Chohan*

# In The Beginning and Now

## by The Maha Chohan

FEBRUARY 7, 2021

In the beginning of The Temple of The Presence, I, the Maha Chohan, established *The Ruby Chalice Visitations* so that I might speak directly to your Heart, to have that Flame receive the Communion of my Heart, to remind you in your outer consciousness that I, the Maha Chohan, am always near — that you can always count on me! When life's turmoils are most challenging, you can recall our Communion together, regaining your Strength, Courage, Patience, reestablishing Purity and Harmony and all of the God Qualities that I advocate.

It is important for you to have this reminder, for these God Qualities are the building blocks of the Virtues of the Christ. And without these Virtues taking hold of your outer vehicles and allowing for the Flame upon the Altar of your Heart to command life's journey, you are simply buffeted about by the listing of the winds of human consciousness, the waters of emotional tides, and the dis-ease that you allow to settle into your physical body. You cannot forget your firm foundation which is your Communion with your own Mighty I AM Presence. For that is where you establish the Divine Momentum of Will to keep striving, keep loving, keep expanding your conscious awareness of God, keep filling your Chalice with the Light of the Mighty I AM Presence so that you are never found wanting.

Your Chalice is intended to be charged with the Light that your Presence determines that you need at any given time. For that to occur there must be a figure-eight flow established with your own Heart Flame connecting consciously with the Heart of your Presence and establishing the Mind of God where you are. That Mind knows what you need, knows every situation of your present life, knows the future as it stands at that moment, given the circumstances and the attainment that you have garnered. As that attainment and mastery in the Light of God is expanded, your future is also expanded and takes on new opportunity, new awareness of the Mighty I AM. It is then that you truly realize that the Mighty I AM Presence is the All-in-All of your Being!

It is my role as the Maha Chohan, as well as all of the Chohans of each of the Rays, to teach, instruct, guide, guard, direct, and sustain those who are the sincere disciples of the Mighty I AM Presence — those striving toward God and opening their Heart's Chalice to receive more of the Presence of God. Many of you have had your own personal Initiations and cycles directly with one or more of these Chohans or myself. You could witness in your book of Christhood to that which you have come to know as the Truth of the Law that has held you firmly fixed in the Vibration and Charge of Light that enables your overcoming, your acceleration, and yes, blessed ones, the peaceful solution and resolve of those areas of life that seem to be most challenging.

The previous quarterly cycle here at The Temple[1], having focused upon the Great Silence and your role as the Christ Momentum that you establish to enter into that Silence, was most important, for without it you are at the mercy of the buffeting of all the unreality of the human consciousness, of the riptides of mortal thought and feeling flying hither and yon.

*For you must have a charged atmosphere of Ascended Master Light permanently maintained round about you!*

You must have a core of the White Fire of Purity that magnetizes to you from your Mighty I AM Presence your own focus of the Mind of God that is your Christ Presence, which you do require to meet your needs at any given time, for any reason and any circumstance of life! For this to occur, there must be the preparation of your vehicles, hence, the God Qualities that I outline as a way in which you could hone and fashion the Virtues of the Christ.

---

[1] NEW YEAR'S CONCLAVE: *HOME IN THE HEART OF THE GREAT, GREAT SILENCE*, DECEMBER 28, 2020 - JANUARY 1, 2021

Recognizing that there are those novices who will read my words, who come with their inherent tendency to procrastinate, to rebel against any authority — whether it be their own God Presence or merely a voice on the street — matters not. There are those whose human ego has decided that it knows best. If you approach Us with such afflictions, until there is the transmutation of the records that have been woven round about your outer vehicles, the human will, the human ego, the human desires, there will always be a fight, a struggle that goes on within your members. Each time the Light comes forth and approaches that unreality that still remains, it will rise up, sensing that it has been challenged by the Light, knowing that the Light will ultimately prevail, and yet it insists upon stirring the emotions, thinking negative thoughts, perpetuating dis-ease.

This is why, blessed ones, you must garner the Light of God in your spiritual centers. You must invoke the Light so that it can displace, transmute, and leave the pure record that is the Divine Intent of your Mighty I AM Presence for your lifestream. For never was it the plan that you would be lacking in that Purity, that Divine Direction, that opportunity to engage with the Presence of God, moment by moment. When you finally grasp that Truth of Cosmic Law®, your life will change. The acceleration of Light will begin to build up and you will transmute those records, putting them into the Flame, no longer trying to hold on to them by the human ego or the human desires.

Instead, you will cause the Fullness of the Patterns of the God Qualities streaming forth as Light and Momentum from your own Mighty I AM Presence to saturate your vehicles of consciousness! When you decree *"Mighty I AM Presence, charge and fill my feeling world with your Great Ascended Master Peace, etc,"* this is the action that takes place! To literally penetrate the cell structure of your physical body to move you as the Energy of God's Power in motion, to allow for the clarity of mind of your own Mighty I AM Presence as the Christ Mind to take command at every turn!

> When you finally grasp that Truth of Cosmic Law®, your life will change.

There are those in some religious circles who think they only need to set aside one day of the week for the Sabbath and "Keep it Holy." But I say: "Keep each day, each hour, each moment, Holy in the Name of God!" For that is the intent of Life itself — to come forth, accelerate that Light and Momentum of God, and return in the Ascension in the Light, having fulfilled the Divine Destiny of your Presence!

The rebellious nature of most of mankind is fed by fear of the unknown welling up inside that cannot be explained on paper or by experiment, or it is fed by fear of impure things that cannot be seen and yet exist,

> Keep each day, each hour, each moment, Holy in the Name of God!

for the naked eye of physical sight cannot penetrate those intermediate realms. Such things, blessed ones, feed into the consciousness of those who willfully doubt and therefore sow the seeds of separation, of duality, and of loss.

Whereas those stalwart ones who have firmly embraced their Mighty I AM Presence have opened their Heart Flame as a Chalice upraised to receive the Mighty I AM and are living a life that guards against the misuse of any of the precious resources of the Mighty I AM Presence given unto their outer vehicles. These lifestreams do receive new opportunity in life. They are enriched beyond measure simply by abiding always in the Presence of the Mighty I AM, having the overshadowing of their Holy Christ Presence actively knitting together the Great Silence with their conscious awareness. All this, blessed ones, is the Ascended Master Way that life is to be lived.

Many are sometimes asked: "If you could go back to the day before you were reminded by Us of the Truth of your Identity as the Mighty I AM Presence and the Threefold Flame that abides upon the Altar of your Heart, would you go back? Would you wash it all away, forgetting that the Presence of God is so near? Would

# In The Beginning and Now

you desire to continue where you were in those times before the dawning remembrance of the wonderful Truth of your Identity?"

No one wishes to go back. For once you have felt the Light of God streaming forth, once you have experienced the overshadowing of your Holy Christ Presence, the Charge of Light scintillating the very cells of the physical body that you wear, once you have the clarity of mind to know exactly what must occur, whether it be to your ego's liking or not, once these transformations and so many more begin to take place, you realize there is no other life worth living! *This is the life that you have chosen!*

And if you are yet to experience some or all of these things that I, the Maha Chohan, have spoken of — stay the course! For in time you will. For the willingness of your Heart to engage in the receipt of the Discourses and Dictations from the Ascended and Cosmic Beings, the Light and Momentum that streams forth from their Countenance to bless your lifestream, the Great Dispensations from the Lords of Karma and the Cosmic Councils — all of this, blessed ones, will eventually allow you to have the Fullness of these Divine Experiences, if you stay the course.

It is only those dilettantes who use all manner of human excuse, who fade away into the night, thinking somehow they'll stumble upon their own path. For after all, the Masters have said that eventually all will return home. But have you calculated in that 'human' consciousness how long it will take you? How many incarnations wandering in the wilderness? What will be your choices if not Divinely Directed by your own Christ Mind?

For merely because you know of the Mighty I AM Presence and the Holy Christ Presence — if there is a *severing* that *you consciously* engage and *forcibly* put into motion — by Law, the Holy Christ Presence must recede. And until you are ready, until the Heart Flame has been allowed to open and make the call, you will be moving through life under your own karmic momentums of your outer consciousness. Oh, occasionally there may be those cycles where the Blessing and the Mercy of God will intercede on your behalf to see if there is a Spark of Light there to awaken! And if not, there may well be quite some time transpire before another intercession.

Cosmic Law, blessed ones, is no respecter of persons. You have heard this now for a very long time. It is because the Law of Octaves does not allow for the overriding of free will. And when you establish a strong momentum of will that is not fired by the Flame of the Will of God, is not in alignment with that Vibration that allows for the Fullness of the transfer of the Power of God, then, blessed ones, it will arrest the forward momentum of your acceleration on the Path.

I have spoken of this, not so much for the very Faithful whom I know well are holding high the Torch of their own Flame, but I speak to those who are novices — perhaps never having heard before of the Teaching of the Ascended and Cosmic Beings and therefore cannot know of the Mighty I AM Presence, as yet, in their outer consciousness. Far too many think that it is a badge of honor to struggle in life, when in reality, the Presence has never asked of you to struggle. Even your returning karma can be balanced and transmuted by giving daily the Violet Flame Decrees, by invoking the Emerald Matrix, by sending forth the Ruby Fire.

> The Presence has never asked of you to struggle.

So you see, blessed ones, your Presence and The Great I AM have provided the solution to all of the accumulation of the mass karma that has occurred and how to deal with it, how to put it into the Flame, so that Purity can return to the land and allow for the Flame upon the Altar of the Heart to speak, to hear, to feel through the outer vehicles, as the Light of God having prepared them uses these vehicles to move through life in accordance with the Divine Will and Destiny of the Mighty I AM Presence of that one.

Throughout the ages, you have had the opportunity to live all manner of lives — great wealth, great poverty, moderation, hardship, ease, toil. And yet, here you are spiritually awakened and illumined in this incarnation.

For you have realized by the Flame upon the Altar of your Heart that the very Presence of God is worth your all, given freely to the Mighty I AM — your love, your communion, the very Presence that you draw forth in your day-to-day life. For there is no other life that you would elect to live!

And this really is where you make the most momentous decision of all your many lifetimes. Will you be a candidate for your Ascension at the close of this lifetime? Or will you be among those who will reincarnate — one, two, three or more times — to learn more lessons, to put more things into the Flame that could have been put into the Flame in this incarnation?

The *false identity* of the karmic records that have created the not-self over many incarnations is most tenacious to transmute and surrender! But knowing that and the fact that you *can* transmute it, it *can* go into the Flame, should bring you great Comfort! For at the moment and cycle that you approach that serpentine vibration — that Gordian knot of unreality — the Light of God goes to work thread-by-thread, untangling the Gordian knot and transmuting it, charging the Ruby Fire into the record until there is no residual energy remaining.

> The very Presence of God is worth your all.

## In The Beginning and Now

Most of mankind likes to relive their human history, thinking that somehow it will help them avoid striving for God Perfection in all activities and expressions of life ever again. But, blessed ones, each time you utilize the power of thought, the power of the Spoken Word, the power of the energy of your emotions to feed new life into an old record that has probably already been transmuted because you have called it forth to go into the Flame, then, blessed ones, you are feeding fresh new energy from your own Mighty I AM Presence into that record — compounding your problems and creating more to clean up, more to transmute, more to put into the Flame.

*Trust your Mighty I AM Presence! Trust the Chohans!* Allow for one hundred percent of the records that you put into the Flame to be gone! If there is an underlying record that was not transmuted and comes up again for transmutation — you apply the Law once more, invoking the Flame of God, and allowing the Flame to deal with that returning record, and then be about your business that is the business, blessed ones, of living the life of the Christ. This is your Destiny!

There are many avenues of life and professions that you can engage in. But the Truth of your Destiny is to walk the Earth in the Christ Light — unfurling the Flame upon the Altar of the Heart and establishing the Current and Momentum of your own God Presence that is always ready and able. For at a moment's notice, the Presence can send forth the Ray of Light to engage in your vehicles of consciousness, the atmosphere around you. You know not how much your Presence is already doing for you daily because of the decrees that you give at your altar. Many of you keep Archangel Michael's Angels most busy! Likewise, the Violet Flame Angels! But establishing the figure-eight flow with the Mighty I AM Presence and entering into the Great Silence strengthens the core of your Identity in God, allowing these outer vehicles to be *firmly committed* to the chosen path of your free will.

> I invite you always to establish permanent Communion with my Heart!

I, the Maha Chohan, during this *Visitation* of the Ruby Chalice, invite you always to establish permanent Communion with my Heart! For I will not depart from you. Your Presence and I agree that you have the Opportunity, and the ability, to gain your Ascension at the close of this life — if you do not hold back, but allow the All-in-All of your true Individualized Presence of God to fill your Chalice and keep you all your days!

*Let the Fullness of the Light of God be ever with you, and in you, to guide, guard and direct you in the Presence of God!*

*The Maha Chohan*

In The Beginning and Now

16

# A New Era and A New Dispensation
## by El Morya

Beloved Brothers and Sisters,

It is with great Joy that I, El Morya, come to you, announcing a new Dispensation from the *Entire Spirit of the Brotherhood of Light* to unascended mankind. Through the kindness and sponsorship of our Lord the Maha Chohan, the Ascended Masters have once again taken up the Torch of an unbroken stream of communication with their unascended brethren. We are eternally grateful to the Maha Chohan for taking on the responsibility for the release from the Ascended Master Octave of *The Ruby Chalice Visitations*, which shall come forth in the Love and the intonation of the Heartbeat of the Godhead.

Let me emphasize that these *Visitations* are not simply transcriptions of the live Dictations of the Ascended Masters previously delivered as formal addresses to their students and the general public. Rather imagine if you will, the Maha Chohan sitting with pen in hand and composing each *Visitation* with each of you in mind. Each

## A New Era

letter is intended by Us to be for each of you a personal interview where you step into the Inner Electronic Circle of the Master, wrapped for a time in the Radiant Mantle of his Ascended Presence.

Do not underestimate the efficacy of this open line of communication. Over the precious *Thread of Contact* afforded by the *Visitation* will pass to your consciousness unspoken insight about the current course of your worldly labors and affairs, and as regards the spiritual work pledged and undertaken at Inner Levels by your lifestream.

*The Ruby Chalice Visitations* are intended by the Brotherhood to be intimate Upper Room experiences where you as a disciple may receive the Substance and Life of the Ascended Master Consciousness. The *Visitations* represent an extraordinary opportunity for each aspirant to receive firsthand the Fiery Love of the Master, sealing you in his Peace and sending you forth buoyed by the joyous realization of your own conscious contact with that Radiant Living Presence.

When you open the chapter on each *Visitation,* understand that moment as your time of communion through no mediator save your own God Presence. As you read the Master's words, composed in the immediacy of the present moment, He is indeed extending to you the Ruby Chalice of his Ascended Master Light and Consciousness, precipitated as Liquid Light. Simple as the words may appear, each and every one is a Cup of Living Fire.

Certainly you will carry the *Visitation* with you to reread many times. But do not deprive yourself of the actual Inner Ceremony taking place when you and the Master first step into the Consecrated Circle of the *Visitation*. For upon the occasion of the first reading, rest assured the Master will focus his attention on you as you read his words, and his Luminous Presence will indeed enter the atmosphere of the forcefield which you have prepared for his coming. Can you appreciate the full weight of his Blessed Consciousness pressed upon you in that hour? You will indeed "entertain Angels." Be aware!

Is not this closer association with you the object of our efforts for more than a century? Have you not desired it? Have you not worked and served for it? We strive for the strengthening of this *Thread of Contact* with not one but many Sons and Daughters worthy to stand in the Sacred, Living Presence. Therefore do not cheat yourself of the full measure of this experience by reading the *Ruby Chalice* for the first time stuck in rush hour traffic on your way to work, or at the lunch counter. Rather, know the meaning of the scripture,

*The Lord is in His Holy Temple. Let all the Earth keep silent before Him and be at Peace.*

Set your personal forcefield in this manner, assure yourself of a few moments of uninterrupted contemplation, open the chapter and drink in the Master's Living Presence, knowing that Ascended Master has penned their *Visitation*

## A New Era

with you in mind and in your present set of circumstances. Enter into this reverent spirit, elevate your Heart to the Sacred, and you shall have such Consolation as to melt the frozen waters round the Heart, giving birth instead to the first rose of spring, the *Rose of Sharon*.

We are indeed grateful that once again your hands and arms are clasped with those of your Ascended Brothers and Sisters. This fulcrum of God Reality in your life shall not be denied. The juggernaut of modern commercial life has met its master. It shall return to its former state as servant to the Firstborn. Having safely broken open this ampoule of Ascended Master Light and poured it carefully into your aura, you shall carry the Radiation of the *Visitation* with you throughout your busy days, reconnecting with the Light of that original release on a moment's notice simply by looking up into the smiling countenance of the Master and returning to your Sacred Labor assured of your own direct link with Hierarchy.

*Elevate the Chalice!*

*It shall be filled!*

*Drink ye all of it!*

*Morya*

A New Era

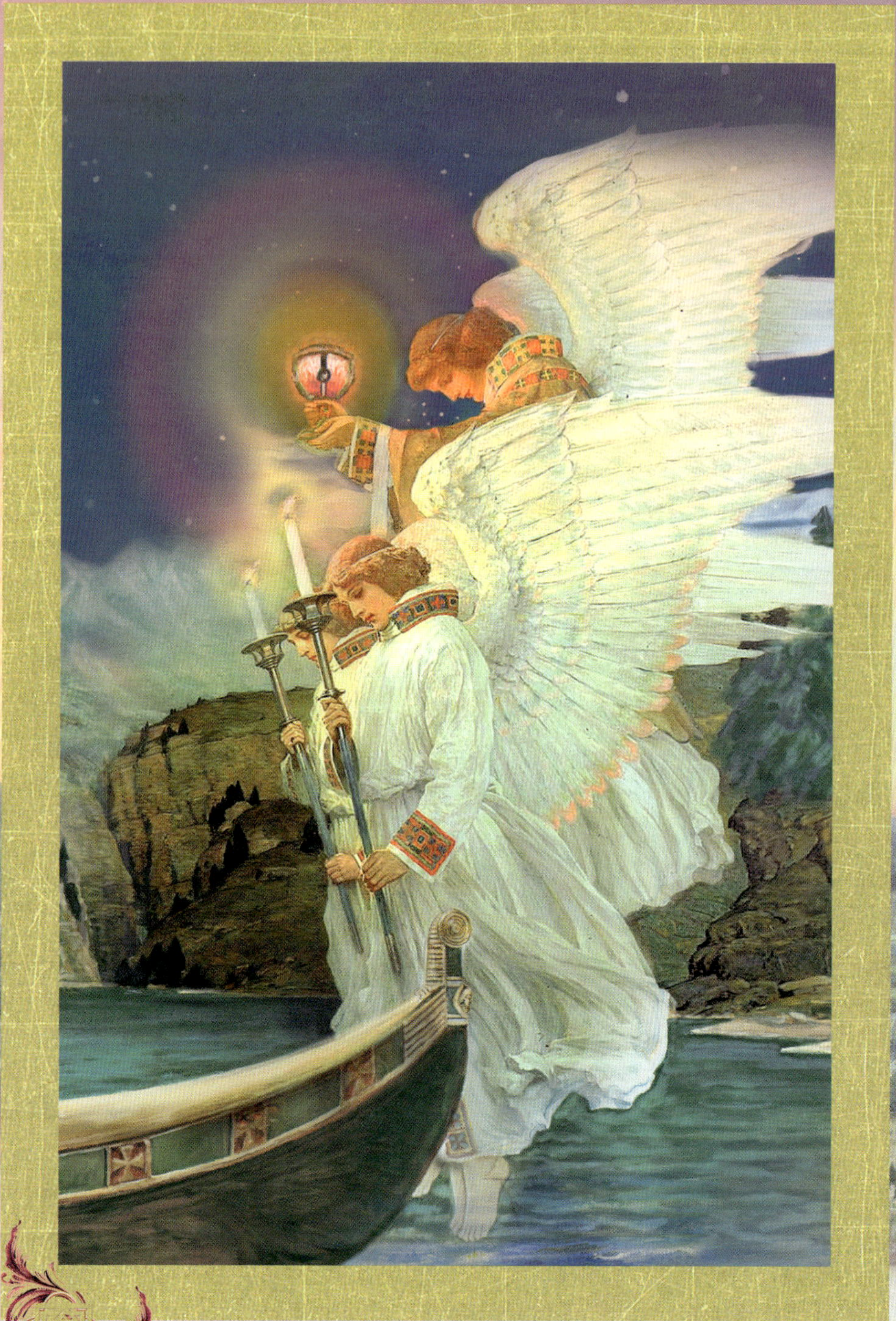

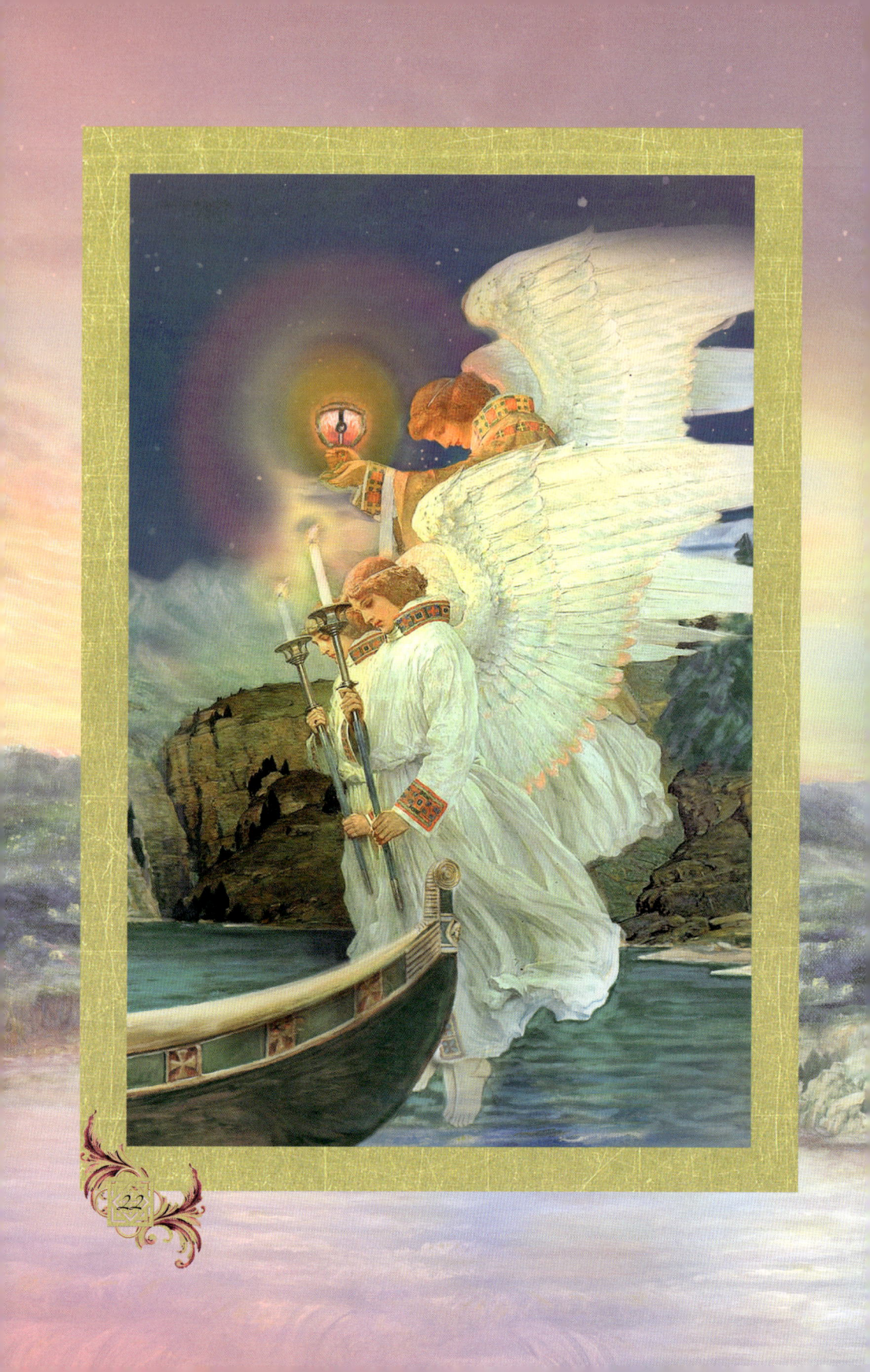

# My Ruby Chalice Visitations

**I** have come to extend to each of you the Ruby Chalice. Yes, I, the Maha Chohan, am aware of the upraised Chalice that you bear. That Chalice is desiring of the Love of God, of the surcease from the burdens of the physical octave that are weighing on your lifestream. Those who are striving on the Path are ready to receive the increments of Light that can be poured into their Chalice daily. There is the opportunity to receive the instruction from my Hand through your Holy Christ Presence, if you will listen. The Ruby Chalice is proffered from my Heart to yours for the Love of the God Being that you are and that you are becoming more and more each day.

There is the need in the land for the *Visitation* of my Flame. There is the need in the land for the understanding of Cosmic Law. Many are unable to perceive Cosmic Law and its instruction — for too many veils of consciousness stand in the way and separate them from their Hearts.

## Visitations

As I raise my Hand, I AM releasing into the atmosphere of Earth, the Fullness of my Heart, that those who are able to look up, to touch the Hand of their Holy Christ Presence, even if only on occasion, may be afforded the opportunity to know a small increment of the Law. This will be afforded, not solely by my own interaction with those lifestreams, but by the support of those in physical embodiment who desire that my Flame shall come into manifestation and shall be expanded. This can be accomplished, only when there is an attention to Cosmic Law.

I have established the regular release of Dictations and Releases that will continue on and will increase so that there might be expanded instruction on Cosmic Law to be studied and taken to heart. Where there are those who receive the Ruby Chalice, they will receive also my *Visitation*. For the Rays of my Heart will be released into the words that will in turn draw my Consciousness to those lifestreams. No matter how many times each Ruby Chalice is read, I will be there.

> No matter how many times each Ruby Chalice is read, I will be there.

These *Visitation*s must go out, far and wide. They must be available to all. If the land is to have the purest Fire of the Ruby Ray Action of Love to cut through all that would stop the expansion of Light in each Heart, individual students must have the Purity of the Law to be found within them. The Ruby Ray Action will be the protection of those lifestreams who do not have all of the teaching, all of the instruction, and have not garnered all of the tools necessary on all fronts for their protection.

I do not believe that, heretofore, anyone has really understood the level of the protection that goes forth from the Ascend Master Octave from the Heart of a sponsoring Master when the chela, the student, the lifestream, knowingly or unknowingly, connects with the Vibration of that One, even if only for a short time. There is a corresponding step up of vibration in the world of each one. In many, the spinning action of the Electrons of Light respond very quickly to the touch of the Vibration of an Ascended Master. There are others who respond more sluggishly, taking more time. You know not how long it will take for each of you.

But, when *The Ruby Chalice Visitation* is placed in your hand, before you even read the words, feel the vibration, for the very paper will be saturated with the pure Essence of the Master's Vibration. You must learn to be in tune with the subtleties of life. For, in doing so, you will be able to steer the ship of your pathway through the straight and narrow and make it home at the appointed hour. Without the sensitivity and attunement you may veer off course.

My Beloved, Pallas Athena, has come in a Whirlwind of Light to anchor the Flame of Truth. I, the Maha Chohan, come in the stillness and quiet of the Heart, that you might perceive, not only the whirlwind action and the Lightning Bolt of Power, but that subtle movement of the Universal Tone of my Heart. Beloved one, the Flame of my Heart is the Flame that you felt when you first came into embodiment — for that breath that went forward touched my Heart, my Heart touched your Heart, and in that figure-eight flow there was the immediate recognition of the Light of God. This is why when lifestreams receive *The Ruby Chalice Visitations*, they will know my Heart.

And, even when there is a course of instruction that is delivered by other Ascended Masters, it will pass through my Office, my Heart, still carrying my Vibration, in conjunction with the other Ascended Master. This is no small matter, when you consider the connection of my Heart to the lifestreams on the planet. I am sure you will find the way and the open door for the dissemination of my Heart to reach all who are waiting to receive.

### *Call to the Maha Chohan and Pallas Athena for Illumination on Precipitation!*

Throughout the coming Releases, there will continue to be instruction given on the Abundance of God and how to bring this forth into your world and into the world of others. My Beloved and I stand and will continue to stand and send forth the Ray from our Heart to direct your course of study in this area. Should you choose to have greater illumination on these topics, call to our Flames for the reinforcement in yours.

Know that the combined efforts of our corresponding Mastery will bring you into the greater awareness and sensitivity to the Light and to your own mastery. When you realize how subtle and how quiet the sound of the resounding Silence can be and how you must listen, you will then begin to quiet all of the outer activities of your world. Soothe the nerves, calm the emotions, quiet the chatter, and you will be able to hear the Sound of God.

The Blessing of Joy We extend to you for the fulfillment of the birth of the Christ and a renewed commitment to the Light of the Chalice of your Heart!

*The Lord is in His Holy Temple. Let all the Earth keep silent before Him and be at Peace.*

Forever holding your Heart in my embrace,

*The Maha Chohan*

28

# LOVE

Dear Student of the Light,

It has long been my desire to institute the delivery of regular communication with you in the form of a letter so that we might have a less formal opportunity to discuss the needs you have in pursuing the Path. I AM the Maha Chohan. I greet you with the Love of my Heart in order that I might be a Guiding Light and Beacon of the Holy Spirit flowing forth onto this page for you to take to your heart and mind, to anchor and assimilate all that is said until it becomes your very own. We will be taking up the Cosmic Law and how you can integrate that Cosmic Law into your daily activity.

Our first point of discussion is Love. Love comes from many avenues. It comes in the form of the love of the mother and the father for the child, love of child for the mother and the father, the love of job, the love of your surroundings, your home. All of these are wonderful expressions of Love. But, dear heart, the greatest Love that you can experience is the Love from your own I AM Presence, your Real Self. People in this time and age speak of "loving yourself." It has become common place to hear that phrase. But I tell you, they do not understand what loving their own self means. You as a student will know what it means by the time we are finished, if you do not already know.

You have experienced opening your Heart to a stranger. You know how good it feels when that kindness is received and that one reciprocates. It is just as easy to commune with your I AM Presence. You open your Heart. The Love flows in from your Presence. And from your Heart back to your Presence flows the Love of your Heart in return, creating a figure-eight flow of Light and Love.

> The greatest Love that you can experience is the Love from your own I AM Presence, your Real Self.

That's not so difficult to imagine, is it? Then why is it not occurring more frequently? Why is it not part of your everyday activity? Why, at your place of employment are you not giving Love even in the most difficult situations? Are you afraid to open your Heart?

In our Dictation earlier today we spoke of fear. The fear of the unknown, fear of making that freewill decision to move with the Light. Or do we not open our Hearts because we are selfish, because we are afraid if we give Love away it won't come back? Because no one will return in kind?

Beloved one, whenever you give Love, even if it is not accepted, even if it is trampled upon, scoffed at or mocked, it is not wasted. It does not go unnoticed. It is recorded, beloved one, in your Causal Body of Light. If you are involved in a personal relationship where you feel the Love which you are giving an individual is not being accepted, be not concerned. Continue to love. For even if this person moves on in their own life cycle, the Love that you have given out automatically goes to your Twin Flame, wherever that Twin Flame is.

So you see, this Love is not wasted. And if we don't practice loving, practice giving that Love, when we finally do meet our Twin Flame, we will not know how to love. The first place to practice, dear heart, is with your I AM Presence, because the Love that you give and receive back from your Presence will be multiplied and amplified throughout every part of your life, throughout every relationship. And you too can feel the warm glow of God's Love, even if on the physical plane your Love to another is rejected. The most important thing I can leave with you is the fact that no Love is wasted. No Love goes unnoticed and no Love is without the Vibration of God.

For indeed God *is* Love. Chamuel and Charity, the Archangel and Archeia of the Love Ray, are the very embodiment of God Love through their Angelic Service. And their Angels are ready with wings of beautiful pink to take your Love and share it wherever, whenever, and with whomever you desire. You cannot love too much. There is no such thing when it is genuine. So, do not be afraid to love.

> The Love of God is All-Powerful. And the true Power of the Will of God is all Love…

You might be surprised at how wonderful life can be when lived within an unbroken Vibration of Love. It is the greatest gift of your I AM Presence. It is the nurturing Love, poured forth through your Crystal Cord daily. Embrace it! Open your Heart! Dissolve all hardness of heart with the Violet Flame. All of the petty arguments and egotistical notions floating about in your world are nothing more than human creation. They block the flow of Love. And for those of you who think it is not manly, or you do not exhibit any Strength with this Vibration of Love, I tell you, you are foolish — for the greatest strength comes with the greatest Love. The Love of God is All-Powerful. And the true Power of the Will of God is all Love, just ask El Morya. He will tell you.

Throughout this Communion I hope that you will take my words to heart. If necessary, reread this daily to remind yourself until it becomes a habit to nurture the Love in your Heart, for we have many Cosmic Laws to take up and to study, but they all fall flat if not infused with Love. Nothing else will matter without Love.

I bid you good evening! I welcome your Heart's fleeting comments. As I feel your Heart impressed upon mine and surrounded by your Love for me, I may truly address your concerns, your needs. Our goal and our mission is not the aggrandizement of the process of this communication, or the building of a personal following. We are here to be of Service to you. To render that Service where needed. We love you! And now that you know a little more about Love, I hope you will understand the true nature of our Love and how far reaching is that Love from the Ascended Master Octave. It is yours to receive.

I thank you!

*The Maha Chohan*

**Beloved Mighty I AM Presence!**
**Charge and fill my feeling world**
**With your Great Ascended Master Love!**

34

# Harmony

**My Dear Heart,**

I come to you this hour in the Flame of the Buddha. I AM the Maha Chohan and I AM wearing the Mantle of God Harmony. I trust that since our last Communion you have been filled with Love. I trust that as we go forward to study the Cosmic Law, you are practicing the art of Love. Today I would like to talk with you regarding Harmony. There has been much said in the past about Harmony. Much has been recorded but little internalized. Harmony is an absolute necessity in your world to open the door to receive the Love you so desire. It matters not whether that Love is a personal love or worldly love or the Love of your own I AM Presence. It is impossible to assimilate Love when you are out of Harmony.

Have you not noticed how your Heart opens wide when you hear a beautiful piece of music — one that has lilting melodies with Harmony surrounding each melodic note? When there is discord in the music you

# Harmony

want to tighten the Heart. You want to close off the Heart. When the chords of music strike a frequency that is congruent with the Cosmic Currents of Light, the Heart opens as the beautiful rose that it should be, ready to receive the Love of God in all its forms.

> Beloved one, you really only have two choices, you are either in Harmony or out of Harmony.

You are saying, "How can I be so harmonious when I am at work and all the darts of the world are pitted against me, with the weight of the city resting on my shoulders, the unhappy individuals who are ready to blame me for all of their woes? How am I to maintain Harmony in such chaos?" Beloved one, you really only have two choices, you are either in Harmony or out of Harmony. We know what happens when you are in Harmony. You are open to receive the Love and the Good that is given to the universe.

When there is inharmony, there is desecration of life. When you are out of Harmony, you make a freewill decision to exist on the plane of human creation. Human creation contains all of those aspects that are uncomfortable, all of the darts, all of the ugliness, all of the woes and the weight of the world. It is your choice. Yes, that is one plane of consciousness and vibration you can exist on. You can move through your day in that state, come home fatigued, drained of all the energy you were given at the beginning of the day, eager to lay your head down so that you might have another opportunity to recharge in the Octaves of Light. Indeed, that is one choice.

But what a far grander, more beautiful, and more comfortable choice to *determine to be in Harmony*. It is a matter of a freewill decision. You can maintain your Harmony if you will but practice, if you will but replace bad habits with good habits. What are those good habits? One good habit you could practice would be to take a deep breath before uttering a word to a disgruntled individual, or counting to ten before addressing a violent discordant situation. When necessary remove yourself from the location, if only by twenty feet. Collect your Harmony and your composure, then go back into the fray, fully composed, fully harmonious.

There is another reason for maintaining your Harmony — not just to receive Love, but to be able to meet discord with the full Power of the Love of God. This does not mean you adopt a "namby pamby" attitude. You can stand in full armor doing great battle yet be in full Peace and Harmony. The greatest warriors of all time knew this secret. They would not engage if they were inharmonious.

> You can stand in full armor doing great battle yet be in full Peace and Harmony.

So, beloved one, you can go through this lifetime in a state of Harmony, maintaining your perfect attunement with your I AM Presence and Holy Christ Presence. Or, you may go through life in discord and live among the vibrations of human creation. When you are in Harmony, your Christ Presence envelopes your being. When you are in action with Purity of Heart, that harmonious vibration draws forth the full God Wisdom, God Love, and God Action of your own I AM Presence.

> Harmony is the key that unlocks the door to the Love of God.

It is impossible for your Holy Christ Self to be a part of your immediate world when you are out of Harmony. The Christ Self must step back and allow you to go through whatever it is you feel you must do on your own. Keep in mind your Christ Self is there to be in action with you, not to be a silent observer. Would you deprive your Holy Christ Presence of that wonderful opportunity of being in action with you day-by-day, hour after hour?

Harmony is the key that unlocks the door to the Love of God. Dear one, I give you a new Beatitude:

*"Blessed are those who are in Harmony, for theirs is the Kingdom of Love."*

I trust that you will practice Harmony throughout this week and all the weeks to come. But particularly put your attention on this aspect of Cosmic Law at every opportunity until you have established the good habits of Harmony. You will forget from time to time, and I understand that you will. But there will also come the time when you will be such a walking harmonious representative of your Presence that all of life will be magnetized to you. All of life will look at you and wonder, "How can that one be so harmonious amidst such chaos? How can it be possible?"

Develop your own techniques to remind yourself to attune to Harmony. I am sure you have something precious in your world which can key you into a harmonious vibration. It may be a piece of music you need to play. You may find you must rise in attunement above the commotion of your surroundings. There are those with a momentum of meditation who need only close their eyes for a split second and focus on the Light.

Within that split second their world can be flooded with Harmony. There are those who may find exercise is a way to bring Harmony into their world and to throw off the tensions of the day. But whatever you require, you must be in Harmony, for…

*All of Life flows in Harmony!*

*The entire Cosmos is in Harmony!*

*The Law of your Being is Harmony!*

> Open your Heart and allow the flood of the Harmony of the Buddha to come into your world.

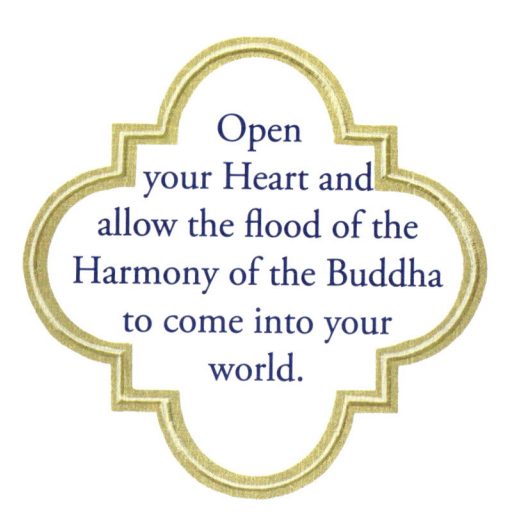

As you read my words in this hour of our Communion, I ask that you open your Heart and allow the flood of the Harmony of the Buddha to come into your world. Feel it. Flow with that Harmony. Be in action in Harmony. Once you have mastered this gift, all things are possible. Peace be unto you. Let God Harmony flow through your entire world.

Until we meet again, good night,

*The Maha Chohan*

*Beloved Mighty I AM Presence!*
*Charge and fill my feeling world*
*With your Great Ascended Master Harmony!*

Harmony

42

# Peace

My Dear Student,

The time has come for Peace. We have had the Prince of Peace. We have had Beloved Ghandi bringing Peace. We have had many world leaders espousing Peace. But the real Responsibility for Peace lies with you.

The Prince of Peace said, "Peace, be still!" and calmed the waters. Now you must say, "Peace, be still!" and calm your own emotional body. It must be as quiet as a calm lake on a still day. This calm is necessary, for the solar plexus and the feeling world are by nature energy-in-motion. In order to manifest the Purity of all you would have come to pass, this e-motion must be clear as a still, crystalline pool reflecting the Purity of God, reflecting his pure Energy-In-Motion. Otherwise discord, anxiety, or any disturbance in the solar plexus chakra will taint the outcome of your creation and the quality of your life experience. When this self-mastery

PEACE

is once and for all accomplished, you shall gaze into your own purified feeling world and see reflected there the clear outpicturing of your own God Vision.

Again comes the Affirmation of Beloved Jesus, "Peace, be still!" How do you accomplish this Ascended Master Peace? How do you manifest such Peace in your world? You must train your emotions to be resolved in every aspect of life. You will always have conflict. There will always be turmoil. Recognize that such are part of the Path of striving and overcoming. But you can meet conflict and turmoil with Faith, with Hope, and with confidence in the Light of God. Yes, the Light of God, the Light of your own I AM Presence will never fail you!

> You can meet conflict and turmoil with Faith, with Hope, and with confidence in the Light of God.

If you will but practice entering into the Great Silence regularly, you will find that the stillness of your Presence will become a permanent part of your everyday activities. Then you will have stillness in all that you do, and that serenity will bring God Peace. True, there is great activity within the Silence of God, but in the Divine Realm all Creation is carried on amidst the greatest, most peaceful outpicturing of the pure Light of God.

You need to recognize also that the greatest conflict you deal with is not to be found in the outer world, but in the warring among your own members. The constant arguing back and forth, "Should I, shouldn't I? Is it right, is it wrong?" Dear one, if you will but open your Heart, maintain your Harmony, and flood your world with the Love of your I AM Presence and the Light of God, you will have Peace in your emotions.

Emotions are an indispensable aspect of every lifestream. Remember, emotion is energy-in-motion which must come under the control of your I AM Presence and Holy Christ Presence. It ought not be ruled by the riptides of anger and anxiety or frustration, nor contaminated by the human effluvia that you constantly contact while in physical embodiment.

If you will but maintain your Harmony and maintain your Poise in the Light, you will not have to deal with the anxieties that are so prevalent on the planet. Then when someone tries to draw you into the fray, you will not respond in like manner. For there will only be Peace in your world with which to respond. Peace, in the full Power of the Light of God.

The Elohim of Peace unfolds a Banner of Peace across the planet that infuses a special release of Light with the Quality of God Peace. Peace between warring nations begins with the Peace within you. It is contagious. It will spread like wildfire. It is Energy-In-Motion so

# Peace

powerful that it cannot be stopped. But it begins with you. The Prince of Peace knew the importance of Peace, knew that to accomplish the goal of his Ascension it was a necessity for Him to maintain Peace.

We are aware of how difficult it is to bring the emotions under control. You do not accomplish it by turning off all emotional responses to life. Rather, the Violet Flame is your answer by transmuting all of the old records, old habits, old desires that are creating states of confusion, anxiety, and lack of ability to hear and respond to the promptings of the Christ Presence. When you have flooded your world with enough Violet Flame and your desires have been purified, you will then be left with only those Desires that were initially born from the Heart of God, and those God Desires will be cradled in Peace.

The Holy Spirit flows in Peace. The Will of God flows in Peace. All the Qualities of the God Flame flow in Peace. Won't you flow with Peace in your world?

"Peace be still and know that I AM God."

Practice it! Become it! It is yours!

You can claim it. You too can plant the seeds of "Peace on Earth" to bear fruit and to bring in the coming Golden Age.

PEACE

> You too can plant the seeds of "Peace on Earth" to bear fruit and to bring in the coming Golden Age.

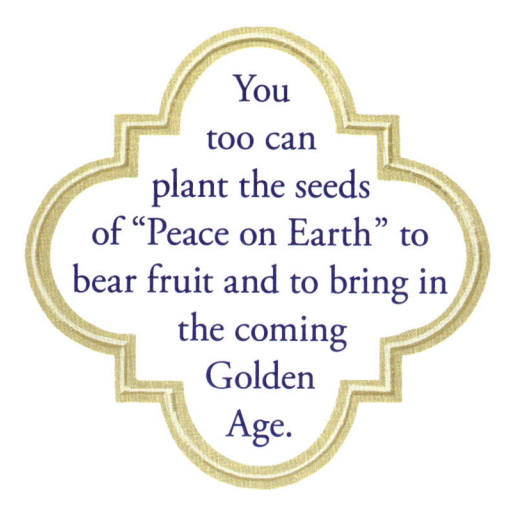

*Peace!*

*Peace!*

*Peace!*

Blessings and Love,

*The Maha Chohan*

*Beloved Mighty I AM Presence!*
*Charge and fill my feeling world*
*With your Great Ascended Master Peace!*

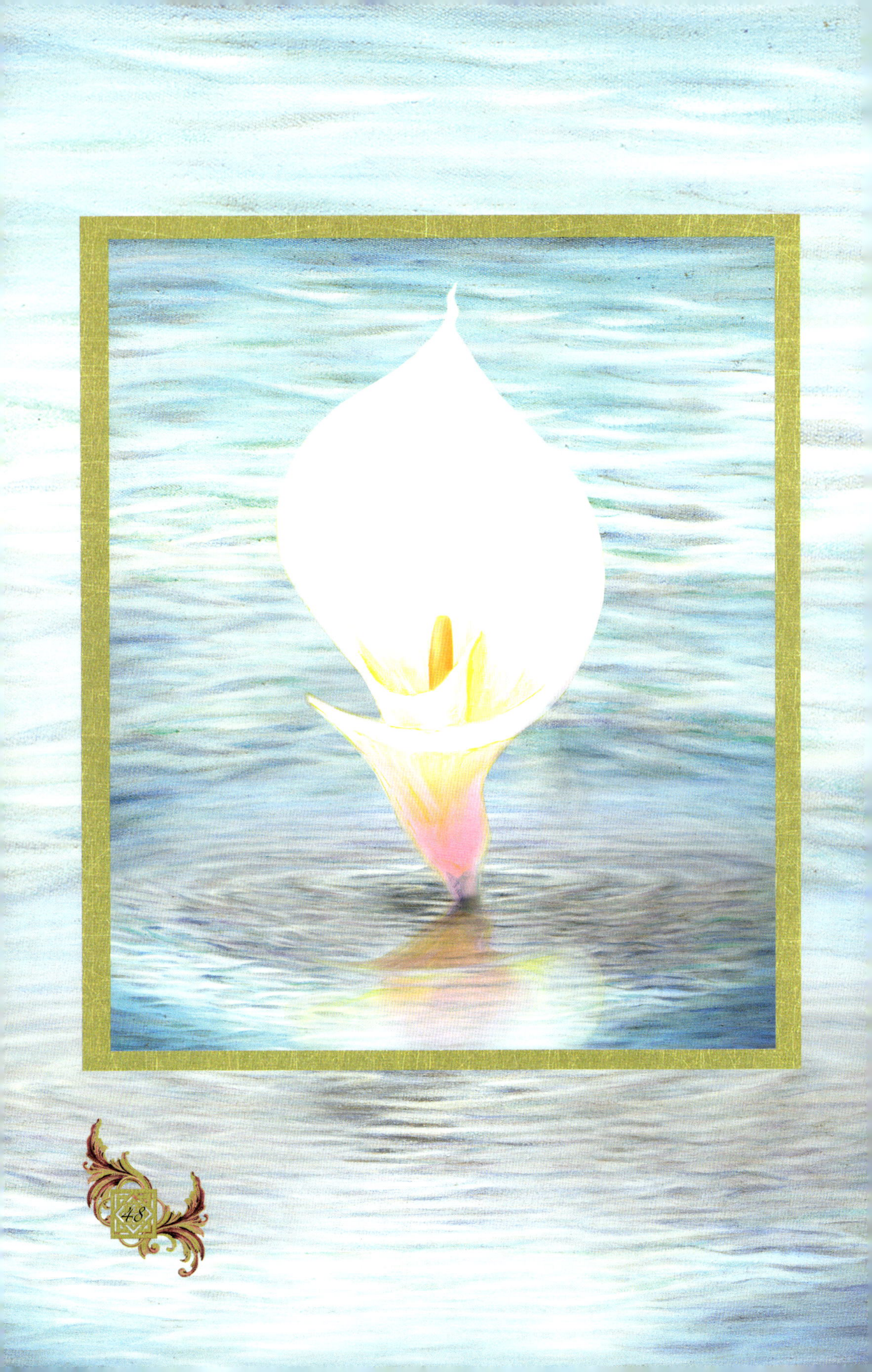
48

# Purity

**D**ear Heart,

I write to you with a message of import for your lifestream, for your spiritual unfoldment, and for the expansion of the Light in your world. In this Sacred Hour of our Communion, will you afford me the opportunity to convey to your Heart the pure message of God's Love?

The Word of God is Purity. Purity in all aspects of Cosmic Law will allow the opportunity for you to make your Ascension, to become One with your Presence, to become so full of Light that every cell will be as pure new fallen snow. Does this sound like an impossible task? Not impossible — difficult perhaps — but you can win your Ascension by practicing the purification of all aspects of your lifestream.

The Light from your Presence is Purity. When this Supernal Light flows through your Crystal Cord saturating your world, your atoms spin at a rate and vibration that

# Purity

provides you the opportunity to transmute by the Fires of the Holy Spirit all karma you have garnered embodiment after embodiment.

The great purifier is Fire. Fire saturating the Earth will raise the vibration of this Earth. Many have thought that Fire would be the destruction of the Earth, the destruction of life as we know it. Those who think in that manner are thinking with a narrow consciousness. Yes, Fire destroys, but only that which is not in keeping with the Light of God.

> The great purifier is Fire.

Every cell of your body contains a Spark of Divine Fire. To release those Sparks of Fire, it is important to cleanse every cell. This can be done in many ways. We all know that what we put in our mouth we become. Therefore, eating the purest foods and drinking the purest liquids are most important. But, in a time and age when it may not be so easy to come by these pure foods, you do have the opportunity to purify them.

Did you think blessing your food was simply a manner in which you were giving thanks? The true blessing of the food is to pass the hands over the food infusing it with Fire, thereby transmuting all that is not of a vibration that should enter your body. During troubled times this is an important lesson to learn as a saving grace for your physical body. Therefore do not eat or drink without properly blessing the food with the Violet Flame. Visualize the action. Center in your Heart and know that the food you bless has been saturated and purified with the Violet Flame.

The air you breathe can have many toxins. It may become difficult at times to take a deep breath. It is important to nonetheless breathe in the prana — deep into the lungs. The body has its own purifying mechanism for dealing with the toxins in the air. Many teas are good for purifying the blood when you have been exposed to air that is impure.

> Yes, beloved one, your Presence, your I AM Presence, can purify your entire world.

Considering all the things of your physical surroundings that you contact daily that can pollute your world, it is no wonder you still question, "How can I purify?" I have already given you the key. Yes, beloved one, your Presence, your I AM Presence, can purify your entire world. Making contact with your Presence on a daily basis is absolutely essential in clearing the chakras so that they can spin at a rate and vibration to maintain your forcefield at a pitch that will not allow you to become a cesspool for the human creation of others.

## Purity

When each individual learns the technique of personal purification by the Fires of the Heart, the Fires of their own I AM Presence, then they are able to purify the world at large. Then it will no longer be necessary for environmental controls. For those controls will be self-imposed by all who are looking out after their neighbor.

We must take up the discussion of consciousness. The greatest destroyer of life in all its aspects is putrefied consciousness. Every ill thought, every discord, every malicious intent — if only of the thought world — is destroying your atmosphere. And as the pure atmosphere is destroyed, the astral plane becomes your forcefield. Pure thoughts are also essential for cleaning up planet Earth.

You must speak to the children at a very early age so that they might be trained in purity of thought. It is more than just learning good habits. One must infuse the thoughts with a pure heart. Purity of heart, pure intent, will nourish pure thoughts. When the thoughts are pure, the visualization can manifest in accordance with the Will of God. Then you will know the Purity of God Vision.

The desires of the heart must be God Desires. And you say how would I know if my desires are God Desires or desires of the human flesh? Again, it is important to infuse your world with daily communion in the Holy Spirit. And as you are fired with the Fires of God, the desires born of the heart will automatically become God

# PURITY

Desires. Those wants and wishes and human attractions will fall away naturally and on their own without any sense of struggle when you are filled with Light. Only the Purity of God can stand in the Light of God. All else is dissolved away by the grace of the Violet Flame. The Violet Flame, God's Purifier, can transmute all that would lay heavily upon your shoulders as a weight of karma — weighing down the cells of your physical body, causing the aches and pains and maladies.

> The Violet Flame, God's Purifier, can transmute all that would lay heavily upon your shoulders…

Again, constant communion with the Light of your own Presence can alleviate the burdens that are not only self-imposed, but that you acquire through the human conditions of others surrounding you. You rise above the effluvia. You must walk and talk in a vibration that will keep you out of harm's way. Yes, the Earth is being infused with great Light. But when great Light is saturating the Earth, great darkness can rise up, creating conflict, wars, and all forms of destruction. Each Dispensation and release of Light requires greater and greater vigilance on the part of the Light Bearers. It requires of you to make additional calls — to release greater Light through your Heart, to hold the balance for all who will be or could be effected as a result of this infusion of Light.

Purity

There are Angelic Beings waiting for your calls to move forward in Armies of Light to deal with these situations. It is not just enough to know that they exist. It is vital to command these Legions. True, the Great Brotherhood of Light is working with many lifestreams across the planet. But each and every lifestream, beginning with yourself, is of vital importance to Us in holding the Flame at your station, your point, in the Antakarana of Light. Light is the alchemical key!

This is truly an Age of Fire. Unlike the fires of damnation expected in the Book of Revelations, We advocate the true purifying Fires of Almighty God. In the gentleness of the flow and the stream of the Light, the Fire returning back to the Heart of God raises and lifts all that it contacts. The only pain comes if you entertain a sense of struggle, or fear of loss, trying to hold on to what you think you must have. Let go and let the Fires of your Heart burn brightly and *purify* the Earth, *purify* your home, *purify* your body, *purify* your mind, *purify* all that you contact.

> There are Angelic Beings waiting for your calls to move forward in Armies of Light to deal with these situations.

Beloved one, as you wear the Light of your own I AM Presence, let it wash your body. Let it relieve you of all the tension, all the anxiety, all the impure thoughts, all of the hardness of heart. Wash in the Light daily even as you would shower or bathe daily. It is a good practice to visualize even while bathing, affirming that you are not just washing with water but with the Violet Flame. Let that be a daily ritual as well.

If you will consciously and joyously put your attention on infusing your world with the Violet Flame, your life can turn around 180 degrees. This process will take place so gradually and so effortlessly that you will wonder what took you so long to come to this point of realization. The most difficult thing you have to accomplish is doing it. Making the connection, making the freewill decision to make that connection and to apply yourself daily, that's where your Victory begins.

And when you have so purified your world that you are a walking, talking Son of God, having been Victorious over negativity, over the gravitational pull holding fast your karma and keeping you earth bound, you will be raised up, full of Light, ready to make your Ascension — never again compelled to walk among the vibrations of human effluvia. Then your Service to the planet will truly begin.

*Purity is a Joyous Path!*

*Purity is a Joyous Opportunity!*

*Purity is a Flame of Joy!*

*Purity is the Light of God!*

## Purity

And *the Light of God Never Fails!* You have my word! I trust that with this reminder of the Cosmic Law of Purity, you will practice all the aspects of Purity that will allow you the freedom of heart to move with the Cosmic Forces of Light at a time when your Service is so needed.

Archangel Gabriel, the Goddess of Purity, and my own Heart Flame are at your beck and call for the flow of Light to reinforce your world. Be at Peace and be in the Love of God in Purity's Flame.

Until we meet again, I AM the Light of Purity in the Flame of the Holy Spirit!

*The Maha Chohan*

*Beloved Mighty I AM Presence!*
*Charge and fill my feeling world*
*With your Great Ascended Master Purity!*

PURITY

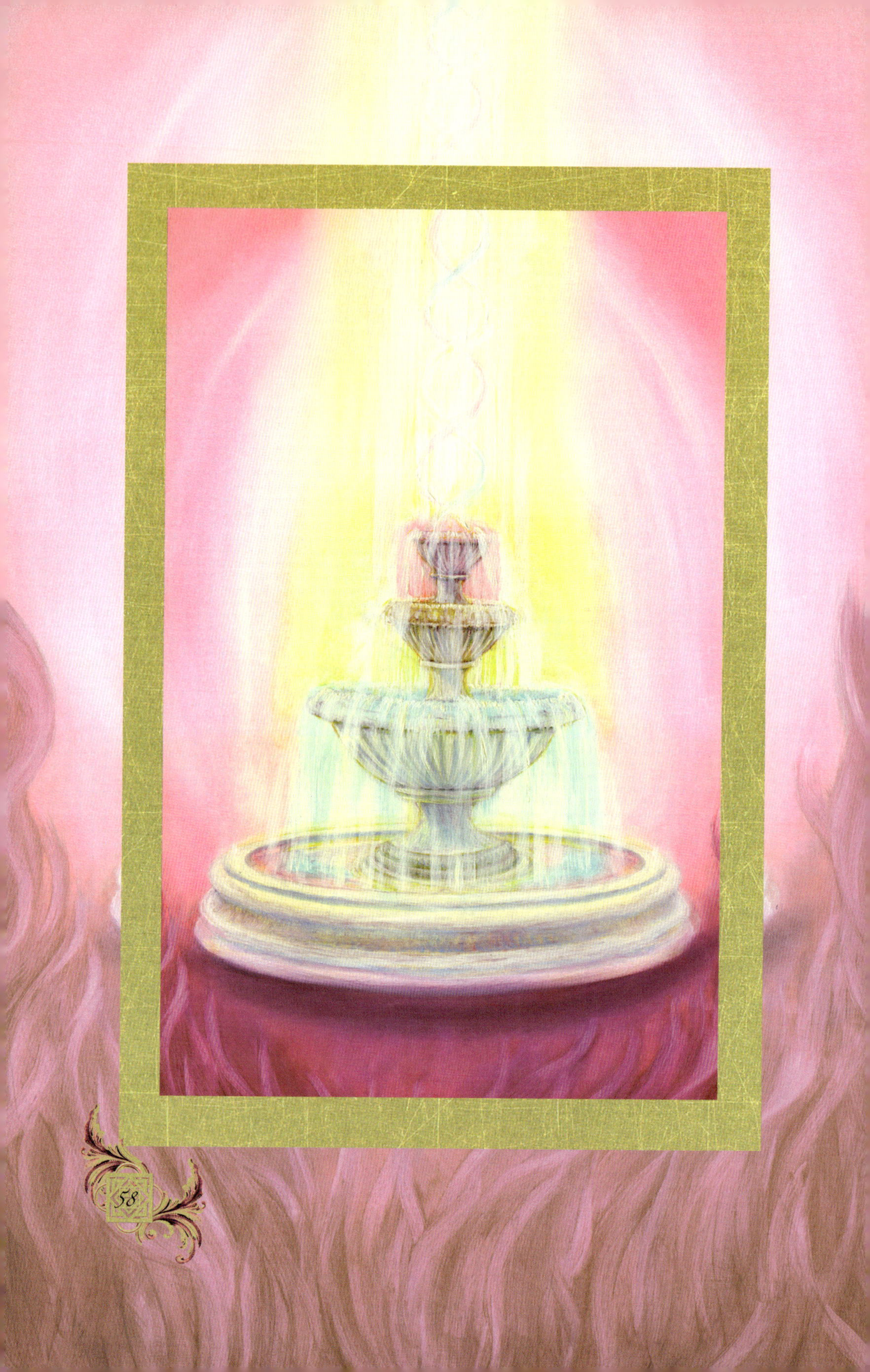

# Happiness I

**D**early Beloved Heart,

I greet you in the Flame and the state of being of Happiness. In our continued course of study on Cosmic Law, I would like to share with you the experience of Happiness from an Ascended Master Vibration, one that you might adopt for your very own in your unascended state.

As an Ascended Being, Happiness has many forms and expressions. There is an Exaltation and Joy that raises the Heart Flame, that allows for God Happiness, each and every time that a chela, a lifestream who has been wandering, finally turns their attention back to Home, to their Heart, to their connecting point with their I AM Presence and the God of Very Gods. This brings the greatest Joy and ultimate Happiness to an Ascended Master, for We remember what it was like for Us before our own Ascensions.

*Rapsodized on what Happiness exists. He gives this example, the most profound that you could consider.

## Happiness 1

Oct 5, 2022

Most of the Ascended Masters working with the planet Earth have taken physical embodiment here at one time or another and have gone through the trials and tribulations and testings before their Ascension. At the moment point of the Ascension there is a release of Joy from the Ascending One's Heart that fills the Cosmos! That Joy Flame nourishes all of Life! And whether known or not, all Life experiences a flickering moment of that Happiness, that Peace that is alone associated with completion of the upward spiral into the ultimate Victory of the Ascension.

> Love, Harmony, Peace, Purity — all of these God Qualities are necessary to live in a sustained state of Happiness.

explodes
continues to be sensed
a ripple goes out
ones
Physical undulations of waves moving through Cosmos

While in embodiment you have many opportunities to experience everyday happiness, but many of you find a point of sadness to dwell upon, such as anxiety or resentment, instead of raising the Joy Flame in your Heart and being like a Pollyanna, finding the good, finding something to be glad about in everything. You may be in a state of Happiness, you may abide constantly in a state of Happiness if you will but practice the previous tenets of Cosmic Law that we have already discussed.

Oct 5, 2022

Love, Harmony, Peace, Purity — all of these God Qualities are necessary to live in a sustained state of Happiness. It is not possible to exist in God Happiness

60

# Happiness

without being able to love, without being harmonious. If you will but remember our previous discussions, you will remember what is necessary in order to ultimately be in the state of Joy and Bliss.

Once you have connected with the Currents of Light in your own world and the Flood of that Light is nourishing every cell, the cells will jump for Joy! They will rejoice! And you will be a veritable Sun of Happiness. Why carry the burdens of human creation on your heart when you have this alternative? When the channels of Light are fully open, the chakras spinning — there comes a stage of attainment when there is such stillness within that spinning, where the chakras become almost quiescent and yet overflowing with such Power and release of Light that you wonder if the universe has stopped. And at that moment, all of Life is in a state of Perfect Happiness, because you are connected with all of Life at a level where only Happiness exists!

There in the state of Oneness with your I AM Presence there is no greater Bliss, no greater Joy, no greater Happiness, for the Love of God is pure Joy, bathing all in its Presence in a state of Happiness. I use the word frequently because I want you to remember Happiness! Happiness! Happiness!

> The Love of God is pure Joy, bathing all in its Presence in a state of Happiness.

You need not settle for less. If you will but flood your world with Violet Flame, otherwise known as the Joy Flame, you can transmute all of the anxieties, all of the lower desires that you are constantly wrestling with. Nothing is impossible for your Presence!

The Ascended Masters are very busy. We are very active in our respective roles and duties with the Brotherhood of Light but we always move about in this state of Happiness. I charge you to give the calls daily to *"Charge and fill your feeling world with that Great Ascended Master Happiness!"* And then *feel* your world flood with a Peace and an understanding to the very depths of your Being of Victory! For the ultimate Happiness is your Victory in the Light!

It goes without saying that there are many activities in your day-to-day living that bring you Happiness. We know of those. But we are talking about the ultimate Happiness, the constant Happiness, one that is steadfast, a state of being that never leaves! It is an opportunity for you to move through your day and outpicture the Love, the Harmony, the Peace, the Purity, and most of all, Happiness.

Watch as that Happiness spreads to all those in your world. It is like lighting fires. You are kindling Heart Flames with the Violet Flame of Joy! And they in turn will kindle more Heart Flames, until the planet round will be rejoicing in a newfound state of Happiness.

This does not mean that one must constantly be jumping up and down, shouting accolades, singing at the top of their lungs or performing cartwheels. You may be happy and still be quiet. Do you not realize that the Meditation on the Heart is a quiet activity? And who could argue that once you have connected with the Heart Flame, kneeling before your altar, that you could be anything but happy?

> Watch as that Happiness spreads to all those in your world. It is like lighting fires.

I am pleased to share this Truth with you and to connect with your Heart Flame. Still, do not think that these Qualities are simple to accomplish. Sometimes the simplest directive can be the most difficult. I caution you to not gloss over my thoughts, but to take them to your heart, ponder them, and allow me to come to you to explain your individual application according to your needs.

I, the Maha Chohan, will speak in the Flame of the Holy Spirit through your Mighty I AM Presence and Holy Christ Presence to you. It is your responsibility to be in attunement to hear my message. My letters to you are a point of training in that very activity. By putting your attention on the vibration of *The Ruby Chalice Visitations,* you are putting your attention on the Heart Flame of the

## Happiness 1

Maha Chohan. I hope that you will attend to my words and make time in your busy life to set aside exclusively for my visit.

You have extended the invitation, and I have come bearing gifts known only to my Heart and yours that will help to raise your consciousness and accelerate you toward your Ascension. Do not allow discouragement to enter your world. I will hold the Immaculate Concept for you, and I will expect great things from you! But in like manner, I will understand if it takes a little bit longer to master each facet of Cosmic Law.

*I will be there for you as you need me. Now and forever you have the key to my Heart.*

Do you detect the Joy in my Heart? I certainly hope so. I pour out my Love and my Joy and my Ascended Master Happiness to you! I will be there for you as you need me. Now and forever you have the key to my Heart.

I look forward to our next Communion in the Holy Spirit.

*The Maha Chohan*

***Beloved Mighty I AM Presence!
Charge and fill my feeling world
With your Great Ascended Master Happiness!***

# Happiness I

66

# Happiness II

Beloved Children of God,

We shall address tonight a matter of great importance. Oh yes, it sounds heavy. It sounds as though it will carry with it much gravity, solemnity, and will be of such a serious nature that you are already bracing yourself for the heaviness that comes with such a release. But you are mistaken, for my words this night are filled with the Love of the Light! And when I AM filled with this Love of *Light* and *Life*, I can only convey it in the Fullness of Joy and Happiness.

Beloved ones, it is time for your hearts to be unburdened. It is time for you to allow the weight on your shoulders to be lifted. This can occur in the blink of an eye if you will but put your attention on Happiness and Joy and Light during our *Visitation*. Contemplate for a moment those times in this very life when you have felt the greatest Joy and Happiness, when you have felt that you could run and skip and jump and laugh with a laughter that would ring out across the Earth and back again.

Recall those special times when the heart has been as light and airy as the bluebird, flitting from tree to tree, singing his song, the sweetest song ever heard. Even the butterfly cannot land long on one flower or one branch for the lightness, the exhilaration, and its carefree flight. Even this brightly colored, winged creature must be up and doing, must continue its forward motion. For there is a mission and a plan for even that tiny butterfly to fulfill. Knowing the plan, perceiving the mission, there is great Joy in every movement of the wing, in every service.

True Happiness, beloved ones, is attained and sustained when you are pursuing the Divine Plan for your lifestream and feeling the Currents of Light buoying you up, up, up higher and higher each day, until the very pinions of Light from your shoulders reach out like wings to carry you above the rest of the world!

The necessary changes in your world that We speak of need not be painful. They need not require human toiling or a sense of struggle. But when you perceive that each change is bringing you closer to God, each opportunity is allowing for a greater increment of Light to enter into your world daily, then what sadness could you possibly endure?

It is a known factor among your scientists there is a certain chemicalization that takes place when there is Joy and Happiness in your life that brings an uplifting Peace and Healing into your physical body itself. Likewise, of course, just the opposite occurs when you carry about the burdens of stress and anxiety upon your heart.

*The Violet Flame is the Joy Flame of God Love!* And this sense of Happiness and well-being can be fully realized if you will apply the Violet Flame into your life daily. Invoking the Violet Flame need not be performed with drudgery or a sense of duty or obligation, but with the sense of anticipation, of recreation — the *re-creation* of your being. And as this Joy Flame is bubbling through your being, there cannot be anything but the sense of Happiness and Peace, of contentment and fulfillment. For the Violet Flame will strip away all the stresses, all the anxieties, all the burdens of the day, and you will be left with a feeling world saturated with *Light* and the carefree *Happiness Ray!*

If you have forgotten how to express Joy, then you should seek out children to observe for a time. Watch the carefree, joyful expressions of their every movement. Many adults feel they are too sophisticated, too educated, too intellectual to be uninhibited enough to exhibit pure Happiness. Somehow they feel that it is a little undignified. But I am here to tell you that the most dignified Ascended Masters ordinarily wear a beaming smile on their face and a gleam in their eye, signaling the pure unadulterated Joy in their Heart.

> The Violet Flame is the Joy Flame of God Love!

# Happiness II

There is nothing quite so disarming as the genuine smile of an Ascended Being! So much so that when you gaze up into their faces, you know that They are experiencing levels of God Consciousness that you have not yet achieved. Yes, beloved hearts, They have realized a Fullness of the Light of God and have attained the untrammeled Freedom of the Ascended Master Octaves! And you may start that very same process in your own life by realizing every day more and more of the Light of God within you and allowing that Light to show forth in the full Happiness of your being.

The Teachings of the Path do not always have to mean weight, or burden, or a type of gravity that expresses as a serious heaviness that you must carry around on your shoulders. Even when there is so much Light present in your immediate forcefield that you feel you cannot move, or your face is reflecting the "tension" of that Light, there is an Inner Joy that cannot help but shine forth. So, you see, beloved ones, even in solemnity, there is Joy and Happiness!

Your ultimate Joy and Happiness will be experienced the day that you make that final step into Ascension's Flame. Your ultimate Happiness is when you are One with your God Presence in the Fullness of that Victorious Moment.

There is nothing so contagious as Happiness. It is much more contagious, beloved ones, than any other state of being. You can lift the vibration all around you through the *Happiness Ray.* Why, even the ability to convey the Teaching is an opportunity to exhibit a little mirth and humor. Simply saying the word Happiness brings Joy to the Heart. Spread Happiness and you spread the Light of God in the Fullness of his Love.

> There is nothing so contagious as Happiness.

As you rise to greet the day with a song on your lips and a smile on your face, send forth the Love of your Heart in the true Happiness of God and you will be in great Service to God and all of Life. For all of Life will respond in like manner given the opportunity. Follow the Bliss of your Heart and you will be happy.

Joyously I AM,

*The Maha Chohan*

*"Happiness is fulfillment in God!*
*True Joy is the Bliss of knowing God!*
*True Love is giving and receiving the Love of God!"*
The Maha Chohan — July 19, 1998

**Beloved Mighty I AM Presence!**
**Charge and fill my feeling world**
**With your Great Ascended Master Happiness!**

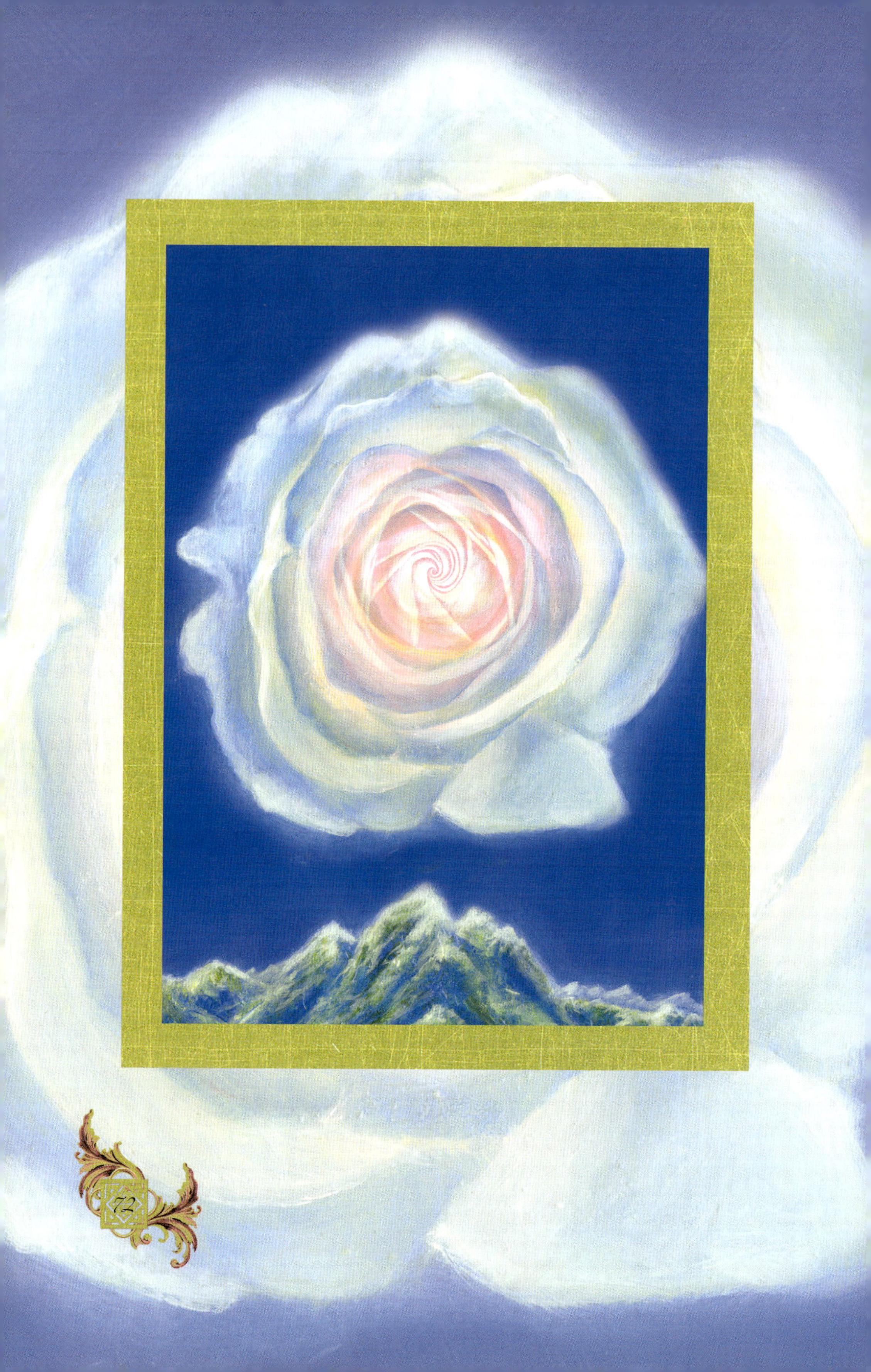

# Faith I

Dear Devotee of the Light of God,

I would like to address the Quality of God Faith. I call to your attention the similarities between your Heart and the rose. Shall we talk about the rose for a moment? When the rose unfolds its petals and exudes its fragrance, it does not hold anything back. It manifests the full release and its essence is sensed by all. Likewise, your Heart responds like the petals of a rose when opened, the full release of Love flows forth unbridled, its Love perceived by all. Some would take offense at such intense Love. They would react by backing away, unable to contend with such Fire. Others would receive that Love, opening the petals of their own Heart Chakra in response and completing the unbroken, figure-eight flow of Light between their own Heart and yours.

You are asking, "What does this have to do with Faith?" As the rose unfolds, it is not concerned with the outer world or the possible rejection of its beautiful fragrance. The rose gives in full trust that all is well and that its perfumed essence will be received in like manner as it gives.

## Faith I

When you bridle the Heart and the Fires are banked to release only a certain amount of Light, then you do not have Faith that your Love will be received. You close the Heart — stopping the flow before the precious Waters of Life have the opportunity to complete their cycle.

Faith is not realized partially. You cannot have Faith by degrees: it is all or nothing. For even one increment of doubt, fear, or questioning will act like the sting of a serpent's venom, poisoning the rest of the release of Faith from your Heart, and all will be lost for the moment.

> **Start by trusting your own Heart.**

How, then, do you strengthen your Faith to be complete and full? Start by trusting your own Heart. Become aware of your own Inner Being. Feel secure, self-confident, and able to hold your head high, gazing out through the Light of your I AM Presence. As you begin to hold firmly to the intensity of that Light, you will feel it consume every doubt and trepidation that could raise its head to question even the slightest Reality of the Truth ringing in your Heart.

It takes vigilance. It takes being patient with yourself, maintaining your Harmony, being at Peace, and feeling the flow of Love through the petals of your Heart. Faith will flow forth effortlessly as it does through a newborn child who naturally has Faith in the protection of the father and Faith in the warmth of a mother's love coddling her infant's form with soft, swaddling garments.

Become as a little child, wide-eyed with wonder. Learn to trust in your Heart with complete Faith. Your Heart, which is God's own Heart, will never lie to you. However, you must be honest with yourself. Is it truly your Heart speaking, or other voices? Those who would prefer to satisfy the appetites of the outer man like to make excuses, saying, "Well, this or that really felt right to me. This was the way my heart was leading me." But you are only deluding yourself by choosing to equate the many voices of human desire with the still, small Voice of God that alone speaks in the Heart. Such delusion does not harm others nearly as much as it does oneself, putting undetected stumbling blocks into the pathway to your own enlightenment. Learn to be honest. Learn to stop playing games with your Heart.

> *When you have gained confidence in yourself, your Real Self, you will generate Faith enough to move mountains.*

It is impossible to reach the highest goals of the Light without such Faith. Every new rung on the ladder of Initiation brings a new sense, a new foundation, and a new vibration. Without Faith that the ultimate goal is attainable, you might falter, as each rung brings yet another new and unfamiliar opportunity to master the ever-transcending way of life, which leads at last to your Ascension.

Your Faith establishes a firm foundation based on the sure and certain knowledge that there are those Ascended Masters who have gone before you, who have traversed each step of the ladder you find so formidable. They are the true Wayshowers — your Ascended Brothers and Sisters of Light.

> Faith opens the door to the Octaves of Light.

We do not call for blind faith. We ask for the Reality of true Faith flowing forth eternally from your very own Heart. You need not be blind if you will but open your Heart, remove the shackles of human creation, and allow the full Freedom of the Light of God to flow through you. Then you will know without a shadow of a doubt that with God all things are possible. There will no longer be any hesitation in your mind or a fleeting glimmer of doubt.

Faith will be a way of life, for your Faith will be centered at the Altar of your Heart, nourished by the God Flame, ready to go forward to be the example, to be the Strength, to be the Wayshower for others on the Path who need a helping hand.

Something must begin the process of overcoming. Something must come first to "prime the pump." That something is Faith. Faith opens the door to the Octaves of Light. There are many keys that will lead you to that door. But Faith can open the door to the Kingdom of Heaven right within your Heart. Heed my words and listen to your Heart. Allow me to present you with this Gift of my own Momentum:

*I charge and fill your feeling world with my Ascended Master Faith!*

Till we meet again in the Communion of our Light, I AM the Holy Spirit reaching out to you with the full Faith that you will receive my Heart.

With Love,

*The Maha Chohan*

*Beloved Mighty I AM Presence!*
*Charge and fill my feeling world*
*With your Great Ascended Master Faith!*

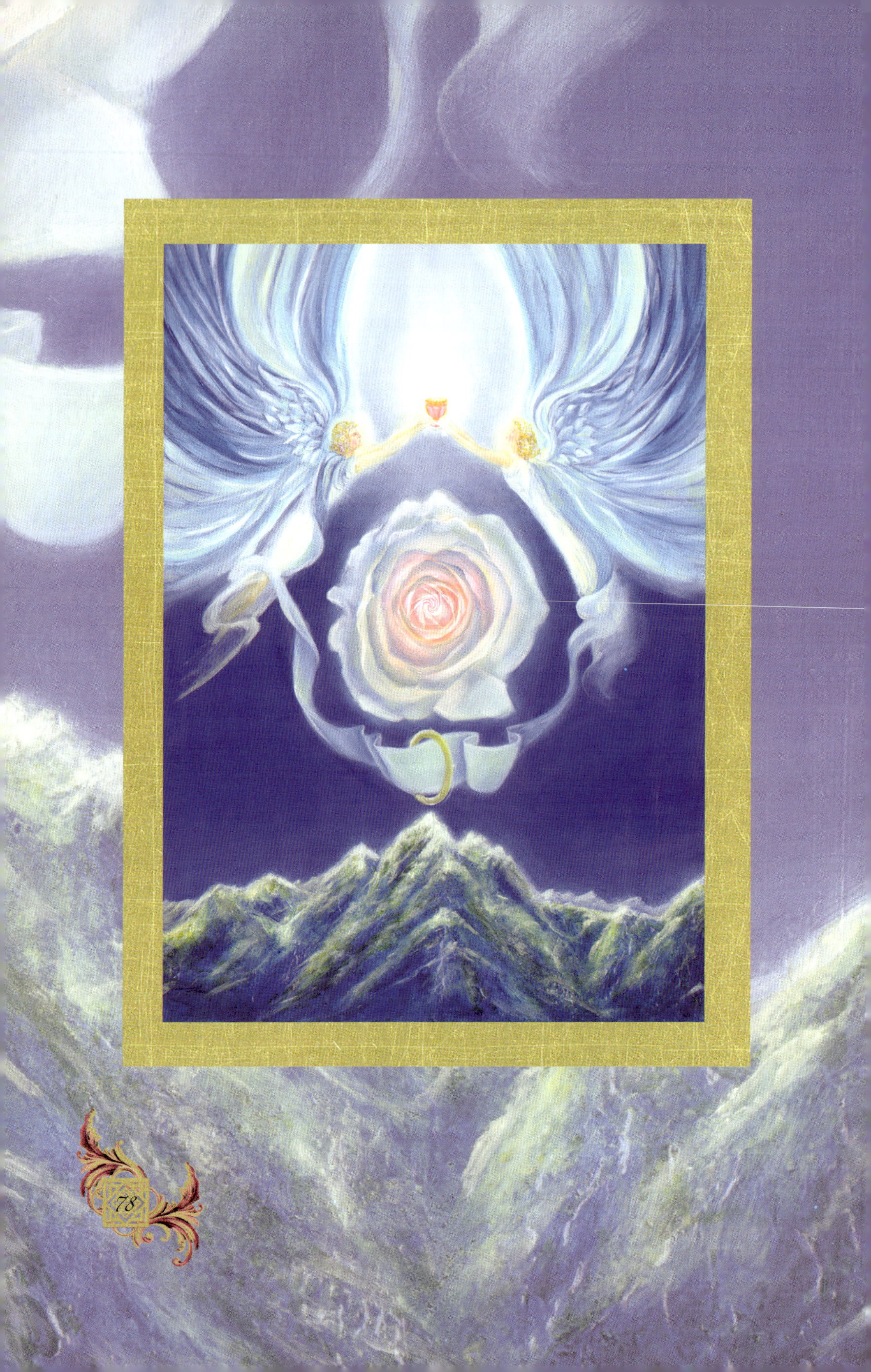

# Faith II

**B**eloved Ones,

I would like to ask you: Do you have the determination to be in the Presence of God? Do you desire to have that Oneness? Or is it only a matter of casual interest because this is what you have heard, this is what you have been told should be the desire of your heart?

There are many who do not understand how to manifest the determination for God. They have tried all manner of application of the Law, and yet there is something within them that has blocked the extension of the Fire necessary to propel them into action toward God.

Beloved ones, the Quality that is lacking is the Quality of Faith. For without Faith, without the understanding at the very deepest core of the Being of your Heart that God is tangible and real, that you do have a Mighty I AM Presence, that the Archangels are real, that the Angels of God's Consciousness can manifest in your world — without this conviction, you do not have the Faith to move into action! For there will not be the Fearlessness that must be manifest to accomplish the goal. And the goal, beloved ones, is the constant expression of God through your being where you are!

The Archangel Michael and the Archeia Faith hold the Divine Office of their Twin Flame Cosmic Light to propel into the physical the Blue Flame of Faith in the Will of God that manifests as protection of all God Reality. Absent their protection, there are many lifestreams who would never have the ability to cognize full Faith in their Presence, especially in their outer consciousness. Faith that would be sufficient to allow them to move into the next day. For without Faith, the next breath would not come.

There are degrees of Faith that must be manifest. It is easy to have Faith in certain things that one has proven, certain actions that one has accomplished, has witnessed firsthand. But what of those Truths of Cosmic Law® that go unseen, unexperienced? Do you have the Fire in your Heart to summon the necessary Faith that you will make your Ascension? That you will become One with your God Presence? That you will be able to balance your karma, fulfill your Dharma? Do you have the Faith in the Law that is written on the Flame of your Heart?

That Cosmic Law, beloved ones, is the same Essence as the Flame on your Heart. When you are unable to connect with that Flame, there is not that sense of protectiveness, security, or Strength that is necessary to mount up the unmitigated Faith that tomorrow is a new opportunity for you to manifest all that you truly are in your God Self.

Admittedly, Faith cannot be recorded with any amount of scientific instrumentation. Faith cannot always be demonstrated by deeds, for there are times when *inaction* is the Fullness of Faith in the Light of God. There are many in the land who have placed their faith in the world's superstitions. They have placed their faith in the hand of others. They have placed their faith in conduct unbefitting a Son or Daughter of God.

The one who manifests the Fullness of Faith stands firm in resolve in who they are, for they know that they are God In Action. They know that they stand in the Fullness of the Blue Flame of the Will of God for their lifestream. And this is the foundation of their Faith for the morrow, for the eternity of their lifestream. The small things of this Earth require smaller expressions of faith. They come easily, come effortlessly, and come with Christ Discernment. When those ponderous issues that loom large for a lifestream are resolved once and for all, Faith can mount up, producing an Envelope of Protection in the Will of God for their lifestream.

Having Faith requires knowledge of who you are. Having that knowledge requires the Wisdom to internalize who you are. Internalizing who you are is the action that is required by your God Presence in order for you to master all aspects of life, to learn all of the lessons, to answer all of the questions, to resolve all of the issues. Thus enabling you to walk in the Light of the Christ, fulfill all that you came to the Earth to do, and return Home Victorious!

You have not just had one life to manifest Faith in your future. You have been working on this for many lifetimes. Yes, you could continue to work on this for many more. But why not grab the 'brass ring' and have the Faith to know that your hand *will* reach that ring, and you will grasp it firmly, and it will be the ring that will connect you with your God Presence!

Manifest the Fullness of the Essence of the Archeia Faith! Pattern the Quality of the Fullness of the knowledge of your God Presence In Action in your world, and you will stand tall in Strength and Courage, in the Fullness of the Light of God!

I, the Maha Chohan, send you forth to become Faith In Action!

## The Maha Chohan

*Beloved Mighty I AM Presence!*
*Charge and fill my feeling world*
*With your Great Ascended Master Faith!*

FAITH II

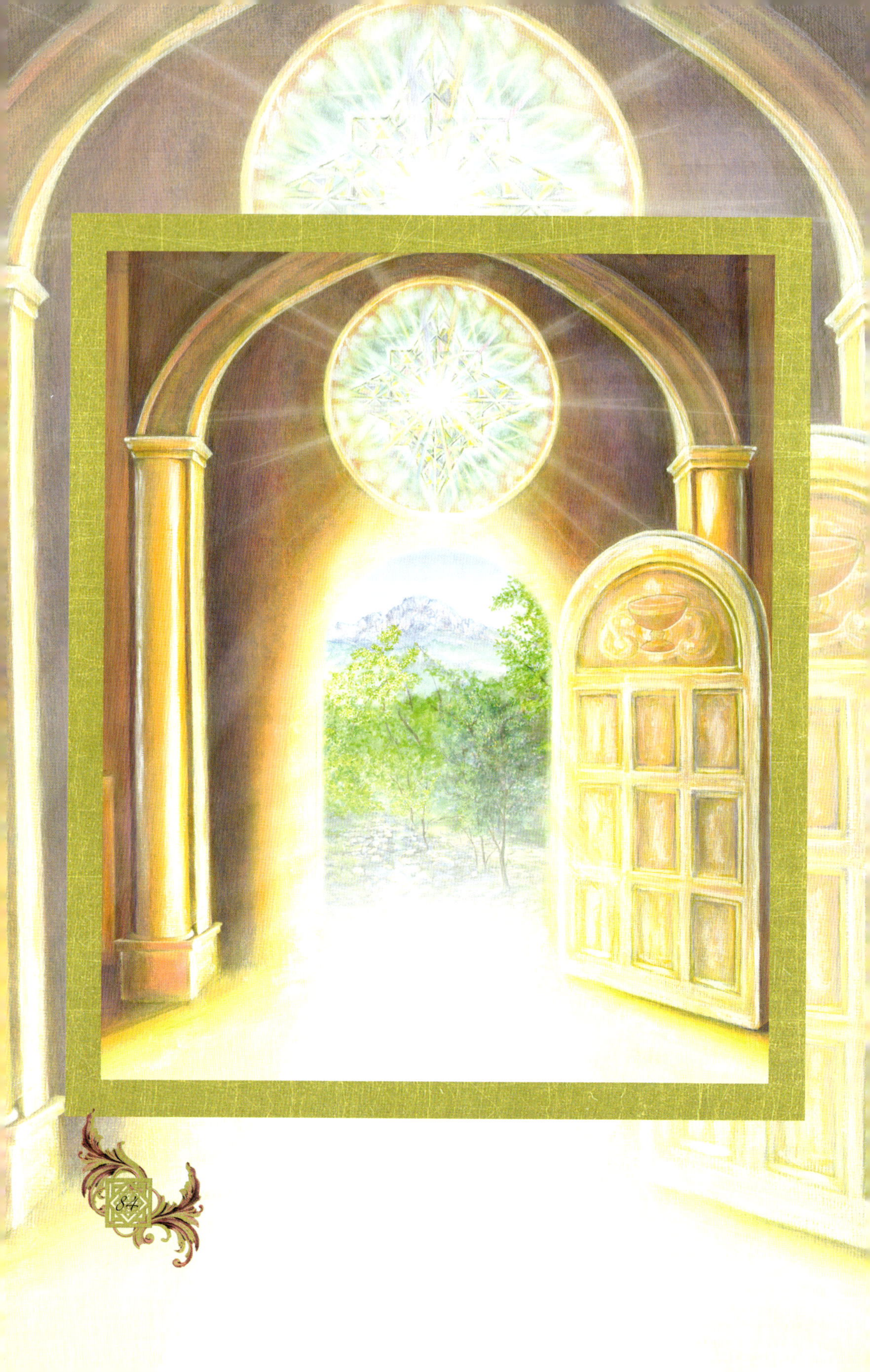

# Hope

**B**lessed One,

All know of the Archangel Gabriel. Many do not know of the Archeia Hope, his Twin Flame. Have you not wondered at the Twin Flame Essence of Gabriel and Hope? Gabriel, manifesting the Purity of the White Light, the Fire of the Mother Flame. You would consider, then, that Hope, his Twin Flame, must be of like manner, of like identity, White Purity, the Essence of all that is Divine and Whole.

Hope extends her Love into the Earth as the Archeia of the angle of God's Consciousness manifesting as the God Quality of Hope. Hope is propelled from the Heart, extended in the Ray of Purity by the Desire of the Holy Christ Presence, for all that is to manifest in the true Reality of one's Being. It has been said that Hope is the Opportunity of the Presence manifest in eternity for your life. For Hope truly is the Desire of your God Presence for all that is right and good and Godly in your world.

# Hope

When there are those who say they have lost all Hope, who have nothing more to hold on to, to aspire toward, they are really saying: "I have lost the connection with my God. I have lost the opportunity to have the communion, the comfort, the vision, the aspiration." In other words, they have lost all that would be desired for them by their own God Presence.

> Hope is the Opportunity of the Presence manifest in eternity for your life.

When one is absent the Love of God through the connection with their Holy Christ Presence that burns on the Altar of their Heart as the action of the Threefold Flame, that silent chamber that is the Holy of Holies for their Being, when that is no longer attainable, when one has become so confused by all that assaults them in the world, all that surrounds them, all that has veiled the Holy of Holies from their conscious awareness, then is when one might say they have lost all Hope.

What is Hope, then, if not the Divine Spark from the Heart that truly desires to propel into the future all that is God Good, all that is truly the Divine Plan for your life? For those with outer world desires who only want to acquire what this world holds for them, securely locked in all of the outer garments of the physical, then that becomes the empty shell, the encasement for locking out that which is the Reality of the Light of the Christ.

When all of the focus of one's life and one's attention is solely on the world of the outer expression of human creation, it does not afford the Heart the ability to truly propel Hope into the future. Instead all is emptiness, vacancy, longing. For those who become more entrenched in this lifestyle, all manner of disease, all manner of illness and aloneness await them. I describe this vividly so that you might understand that when Hope is gone, it tells you your Holy Christ Self is not present in your life.

How can you change your life around and bring Hope into reality? First and foremost, there must be an understanding in your Heart that all that the world has to offer is not all that is available to you. Hope is the Opportunity of the Presence, externalized. You can desire with all your Heart the Fullness of God and by that Righteous God Desire, magnetize every Good, propelling it into your outer activities. But first you must place your attention, place your activities, place your Heart within the Vibration that is conducive to the Holy Christ Presence. This is not complicated. One need only manifest Harmony, manifest pure thoughts, the desire for God Good, and slowly but surely, you will find that your life will take on a new complexion, a new vibration.

As you engage in more and more activities that allow for the interaction with your Christ Presence, you will find that renewed spark of Divine Enthusiasm about your future. You will find that the Desires of your Heart which are pure and right and just and in accordance with the Desires of your own God Presence for you will be forthcoming and constantly renewed.

For some, this experience will mark the first time they will be brought to such an awareness, and there will be a Spark of Light that will project from their Heart into their future. And they will have the wave of the energy to move forward on the Path, accelerated by the Joy of the understanding of the Current of Hope.

Hope is always with you. Consider the little child, hopeful for the gift on the birthday, or under the tree at Christmas time. Consider the excitement! Those little ones are filled with the excitement of the Light of the Christ. You can be filled with that same Light, that same Love, that same Hope!

In Purity the Archeia Hope sends forth her Angels into the Earth to minister to all those who are lacking Hope, lacking the connection with their Holy Christ Presence. These Blessed Angels stand round about to announce to the very Christed Ones becoming that they have the potential to move on to the next day, to the next year, to the next cycle for their lifestream in a higher vibration, a better way of life.

*These Angels from the Heart of Hope extend their Rays of Light and in their presence, convey as well the understanding of Purity.*

# HOPE

At your invitation they are able to hold the balance for you and certain other lifestreams, long enough for them to experience an interaction with their own Holy Christ Presence and to feel firsthand the Joy of true Hope for the new day! The only thing that separates any lifestream in physical embodiment from the Joy of Hope is the lack of the connective tie that they have from their Heart to the Heart of their Holy Christ Presence.

Whenever you are tempted to feel that tomorrow will be too much, that there is no way for you to handle certain situations, that there is no resolve that you can discover — place those obstacles, place those unresolved concerns, place those stormy tomorrows in the hands of your Holy Christ Presence. Allow the Christ Presence to discover the resolve, to discover the new day with you. And if you will practice this, the renewed Spark of Light from your Heart will be propelled into everything that you aspire to accomplish — all of your actions, words, associations. Truly it will change your life. Truly it will bring the pure Desire for God.

> Allow the Christ Presence to discover the resolve, to discover the new day with you.

This is the Hope of your Holy Christ Presence. This is the Hope of your own I AM Presence. For when you discover your True Identity, you will not

> Have Hope
> for the New Day.

stop at only knowing that Identity, but the Hope for your Ascension will forever accelerate you on the Path, until you are Home, Victorious in the Light! And you will be forever buoyed up by the Archeia Hope's Angels because you were able to manifest Hope in your life.

Do not despair. Have Hope for the New Day!

*The Maha Chohan*

*Beloved Mighty I AM Presence!*
*Charge and fill my feeling world*
*With your Great Ascended Master Hope!*

# Hope

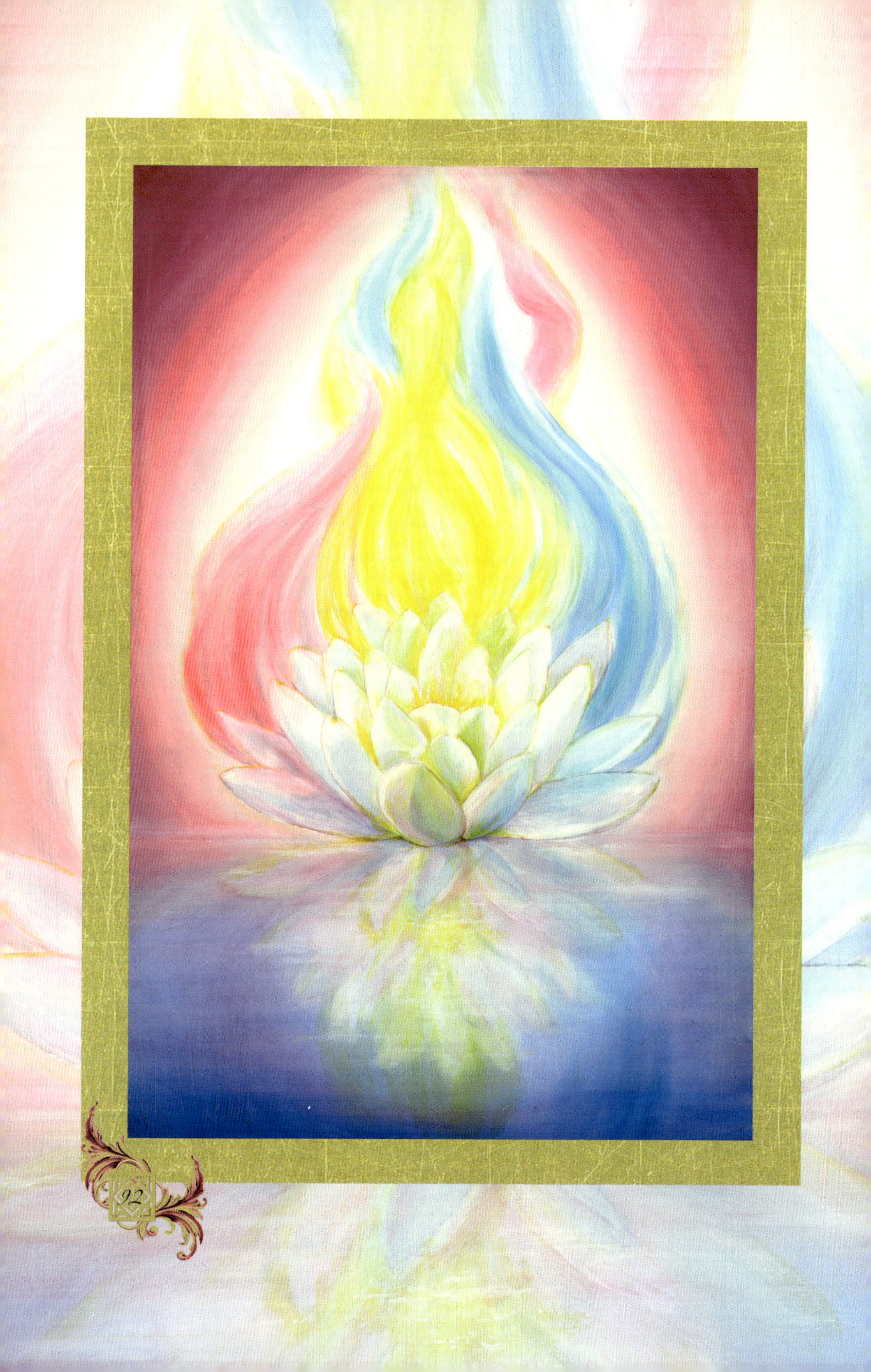

# Charity

Dear Heart Flame,

Charity is a most misunderstood Quality. There are those who perceive Charity as something to be given to the poor. Was it true Charity when Jesus said: "Blessed are the poor in spirit"? Is it Charity when one does not have to give and yet gives? And what of receiving? Is it Charity when one refuses the proffered gift?

I bring to your attention the Archangel and Archeia Chamuel and Charity. Archeia Charity embodies all of the God Qualities associated with Love. Love has many aspects, many shades of color, many actions. The true Heart of Archeia Charity is the Fullness of all that is giving of the Love of God, given unconditionally in every aspect of life.

There are many times when you experience cycles of aloneness, of separateness or feeling cut off from all of your associations, from all of life. This occurs when the

## Charity

Heart no longer is able to receive the true Charity, the Love that is extended to the Heart from every Source of God In Action.

Oh yes, the Heart receives the daily allotment of Love from your own God Presence, and this is wonderful to behold. And for those who have clarity of attunement and an open Heart, this is sufficient for the nourishment of their lifestream. But what of that one on the Path who is just beginning to discover their Heart, who does not yet have the attunement to register the Fullness of God Love and is still dependent on God Love through other avenues of reality?

God Love can come from many sources, many walks of life, many creative endeavors, many expressions of beauty. All of these can nourish the Heart when the Heart is receptive to the pure Light of God. If you find it difficult to open the door to the Heart, to receive the Charity of God in any of these areas, you will find that you feel you are alone.

So let us work on becoming more a part of the Love of God in all of life. How shall we begin? Perhaps it requires that you find a place of comfort, a place where you can be undisturbed, removed from any aspect of the bombardment of negative energy and able to sit in the Oneness of who you are. For some, this will be difficult at first, for you are not accustomed to observing the Reality of your own Being. For the very mechanism that you have established to keep yourself from truly knowing the condition of your own Heart is to stay very busy, very engaged.

The mere action of separating oneself from worldly activities to experience, for even a short time, the Oneness of your own Being will truly be a test. All manner of excuses will arise to dissuade you from that action; but you must silence them, for you are about the Sacred Experiment of the Heart. And for your experiment to be Victorious, you must master all outer conditions that are not allowing you to hear your Heart.

> Your Heart has a most special message for you and you alone.

For your Heart has a most special message for you and you alone. The message will not be loud. You must listen carefully, for the softness of the message is most delicate and quiet. You will find as you train yourself to listen for the sound of your Heart, you will discover a certain peacefulness and serenity. As that is established more and more in all of your vehicles, not only in the physical but also in the emotions and mind, you will be able to recognize how far away you were living and trying to exist away from the Heart.

Is it any wonder, then, that you were not able to feel the true Charity of God in the midst of all the chaos and confusion? Is it any wonder, the beauty and the serenity of the sunset or the ocean waves were not able to bring you a level of Love from God in nature? Most assuredly those personal relationships with the ones closest to you were not able to be fully realized or expressed within the Fullness of God Love, for there was never the time or the attention given to the Heart. Hence the absence of true Charity expressed by that one who would otherwise love you.

Opening the Heart is the first step to understanding Charity. For you can neither receive nor give without an open Heart Chakra. The open Heart is not concerned with how one will love or what one will receive, for it is so expansive that the Fullness of the pure Love from the Heart of God rushes forward and expels all that is unlike itself, not unlike the Fire that is released from the Heart of Archeia Charity. The Angels of Chamuel and Charity's Band come forth into the Earth to minister to the Heart, to separate all of the chaos away from the Heart, allowing for the return to the Silence.

> Opening the Heart is the first step to understanding Charity.

There are many scriptures of past eras. There are many poems of loving Hearts. There are beautiful songs born from the Love of God on Wisdom's Ray. But none are so poignant as the true expression of the message that your Heart has for you. That Oneness in the Heart cannot be expressed in any song, poem, or worldly beauty. It can never be truly described; for in describing it, one would lose all the Essence of the precious protectiveness of that very moment.

> The Heart can withstand any chaos and confusion when it is allowed to be free to love.

So hold fast to your open Heart; secure it well and return often. By returning to your Heart, you discover that it remains fortified and strengthened, safe and unafraid. The Heart can withstand any chaos and confusion when it is allowed to be free to love. The Heart is able to express in all walks of life.

You have now trained the Heart to be able to stand in the Fullness of the expression of Charity in the Earth. For you now have a Heart that can be opened safely, knowing that it is protected by the Love of God. Meditate on this until it becomes a reality in your world that you recognize, and you will truly be God's Charity In Action.

Lovingly I AM,

*The Maha Chohan*

*Beloved Mighty I AM Presence!*
*Charge and fill my feeling world*
*With your Great Ascended Master Charity!*

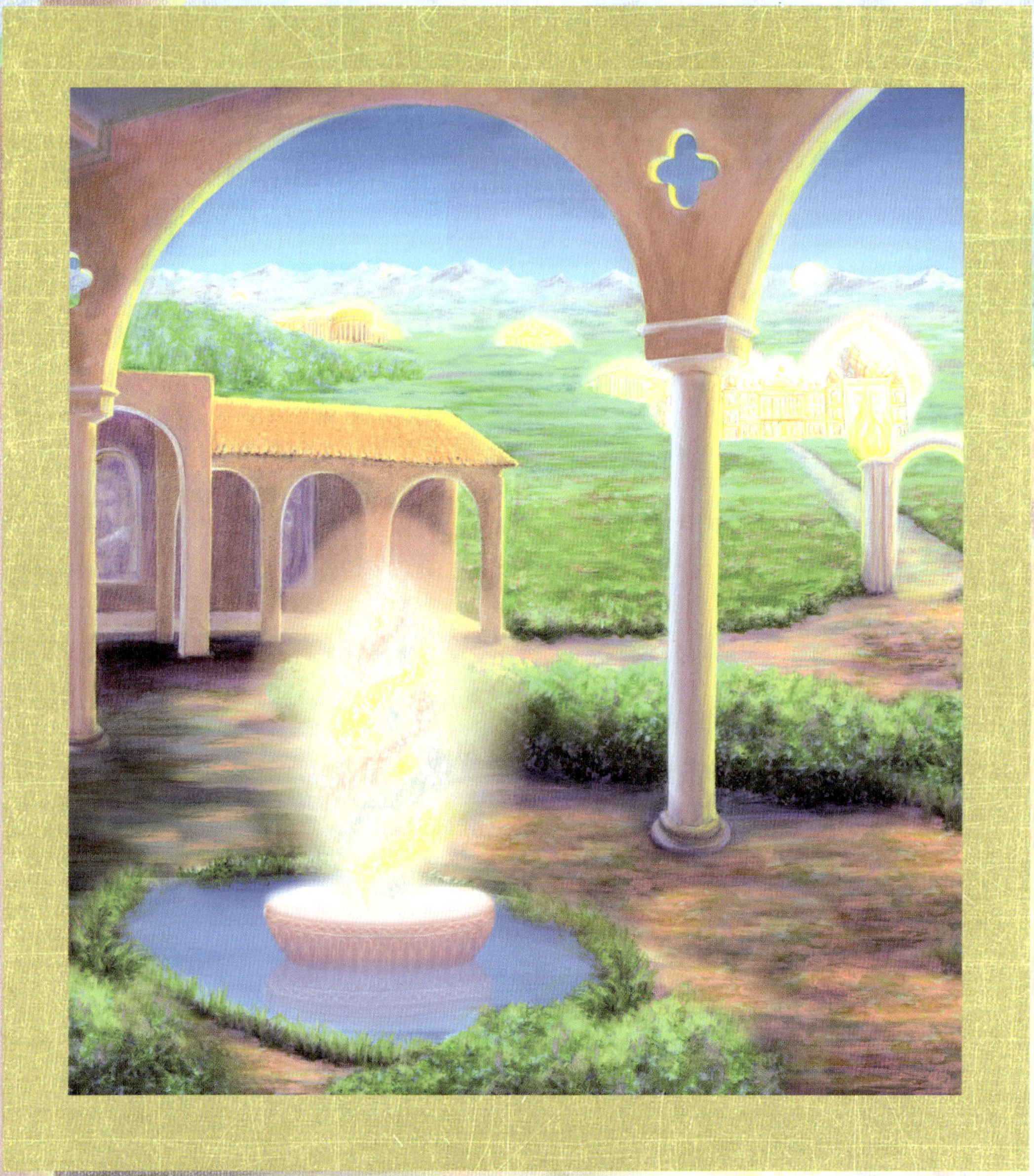

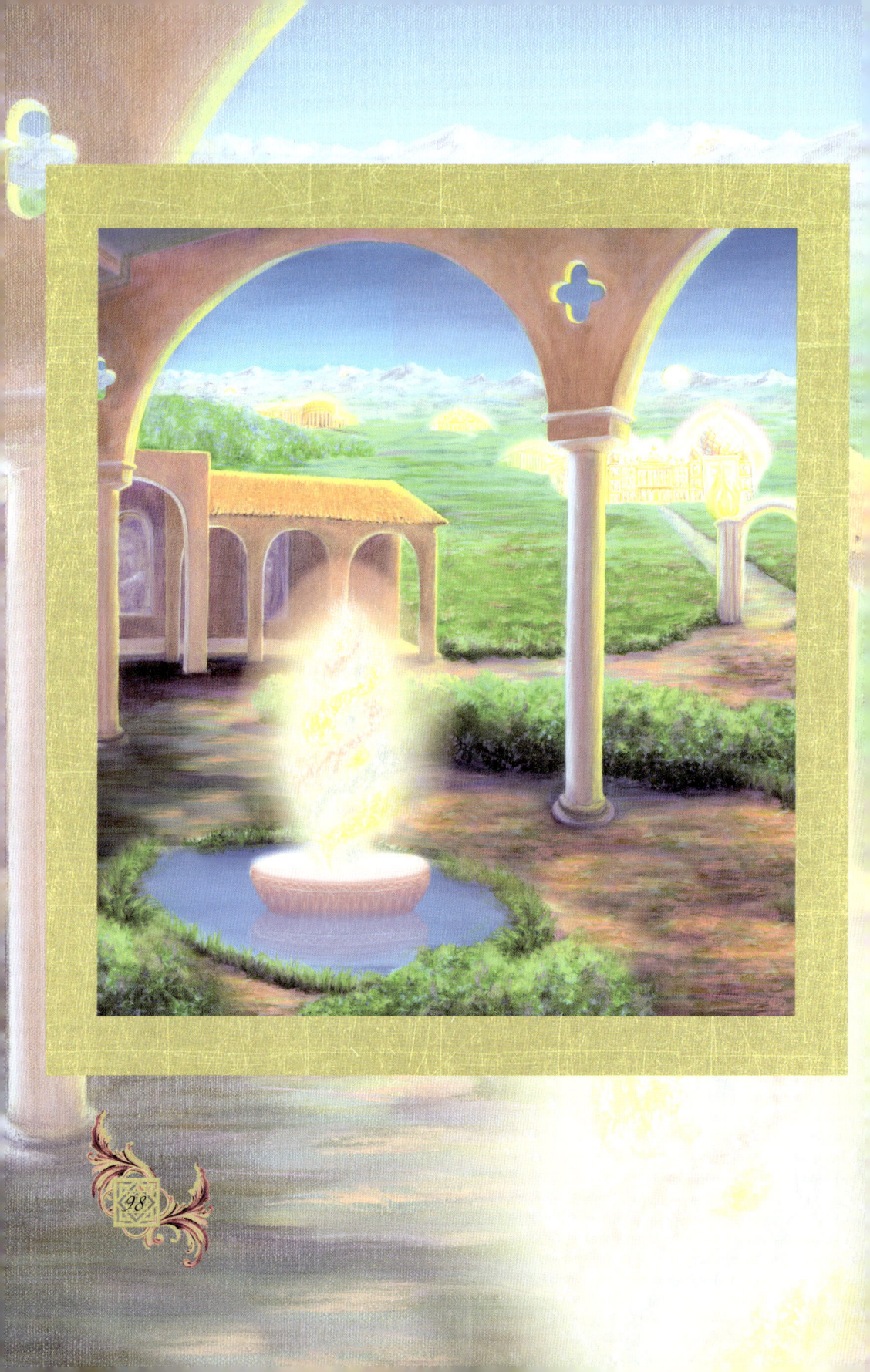

# Patience

**B**eloved Ones,

As the sun has set and evening Vespers are upon us, I invite you to join Me in my meditation within the Great, Great Silence. All things come to those who wait upon the Lord. Waiting upon the Lord is one of the most difficult things to accomplish amidst the modern world's chaos and confusion. It requires mastering the art of Patience.

To sit in the Silence, to harness the steed of the mind that wants to race ahead, to harness the intellect that wants to revolve everything that has come and gone before as well as the plans for the morrow — all of this is difficult indeed. For to enter into a state of Listening Grace marked by quiet, calm, and true Peace requires much self-discipline as well as tolerance for your own existing world of circumstance.

Patience

Remember, you are seeking an opportunity to commune with the God of Very Gods. If you become impatient before even reaching the first door, how do you expect to ascend the stairs beyond the door? There are many levels of consciousness to pass through.

You must have Patience and tolerance with yourself before, during, and after your meditation in order to experience the Fullness of the Light of God. The reward for your exercise in Patience is the ultimate Happiness that life offers anyone. It is the Joy to be found in the full expression of God's Love.

> The reward for your exercise in Patience is the ultimate Happiness that life offers anyone.

Patience is an attribute of Wisdom garnered through much experience on the Path toward Godhood over many embodiments. Those who are tolerant and able to hold their tongue in poised restraint while others expose their ignorance and irritation are always one step ahead of the forces that would rob them of the Light of their own Inner Being. Those who speak impetuously usually have very little to say and display a rather shallow consciousness.

Truly, the contrasts of your own life experiences are able to yield to you insights which will build greater Patience and tolerance if you will attend to the promptings of your Christ Self rather than the constant rumblings of discontent which only impede your progress. When you are "out of patience," there follows irritation, jagged rhythms, and the deterioration of the precious Life Forces of your being.

Patience is part of the natural flow of the rhythm of Life through your Crystal Cord. It should manifest as that state of poised Christ Attunement which El Morya has termed the *Tension of Light*. This is an action of the Light of God standing on alert within your immediate forcefield, ready to leap into action on the instant when directed.

If you do not hold to that *Tension of Light,* if you release the intense buildup of Sacred Fire prematurely through discord, you will find yourself wanting and unprepared to meet the demands of the hour. This divinely ordained release is best likened unto an arrow drawn back from the bow to full extension, the arrow poised and ready for a precise and perfectly timed release.

Harmony leads to Patience. Wisdom leads to Patience. True tolerance and respect for those who do not have the understandings of the Law, even the youngest, will help you to acquire greater Patience. How can you be a teacher of the Laws of God without Patience? Will you become irritated with the student who does not immediately grasp the thought, the concept, or the tension of the arrow you have released?

Perhaps that student will become discouraged and turn away believing that they have failed. Whereas, if you had exhibited greater Patience, the next striving on their part might have been the one to be Victorious when they might have fully grasped the aspect of the Law being presented. The teacher who becomes impatient, who prematurely accepts the appearance of failure on the part of his charges, or who gives up just at the moment of Victory, that one too has lost out for the moment.

One must learn the difference between human dallying and Divine Patience. Patience operates in accord with Wisdom, understanding, and the tangible flow of the Light of God as its foundation. Why release the Energy of God before the perfect moment? The one who abides within their own Fortress of Peace and Harmony awaiting the correct moment to address a human condition is using the conservation of the Light necessary to garner the greatest capacity within their own being.

> How do you discover how to listen? Enter the Great Silence.

Why be irrational and try to confront a dilemma before you can be effective? How do you know the perfect time? You must listen. How do you discover how to listen? Enter the Great Silence. Practice the art of stilling the mind and the emotions so that you can hear the messages as they are released from on high, and allow for that perfect attunement with your Holy Christ Self which will enable you to respond at the most propitious moment.

Anything outside the intent of your Holy Christ Presence and the intuition of that Christ Self to act will be simply a guess on your part. You may get lucky. You may win a few rounds on the strength of your own intellect, and many people hobble through life that way. But wouldn't you rather win and be Victorious each and every time?

I would like to touch upon the correct understanding of Patience in your Path of striving toward the Light. Each of you is at different levels of attainment and vibration. Every lifestream is totally and completely unique. No two are at the same place at the same time. Nor do We expect our devotees to have the same experiences and revelations. Therefore, there are always going to be new levels of attainment that each one is striving to reach. I might add that this process is ongoing even for the Ascended Masters.

As you work to purify the body, purify the mind, the heart, the soul, there are steps on the ladder followed by what might be termed a spiritual plateau. Reaching such a plateau, you will rightly feel a great sense of accomplishment and a feeling that you have arrived. What a glorious day that is! Naturally you become comfortable for a while.

PATIENCE

    May I give you a word of advice? Do not tarry in that state or permit yourself a moment's complacency. Do not consider you have arrived at the maximum you can achieve in this embodiment. By arriving, it is your signal to go higher and farther and to keep striving. This too requires Patience, beloved ones. For many times the student becomes weary of continually trying and continually moving. Nevertheless, in your octave, life moves either up or down, it cannot possibly remain static. Neither can you remain coasting along on the same vibration. Therefore I charge you with the Ascended Master Patience to *keep on keeping on* so long as you draw breath.

    Oh, try to realize that in this spirit of Patience which I AM advocating, you *can* reach the ultimate goal afforded you as Opportunity! Set your sights on the Ascension and you will not countenance impatience. Nor will you fly to the opposite extreme and become complacent about your plateau of vibration and attainment. You *will* keep on keeping on. You *will* move with the Light.

    There is movement and rhythm in Patience, beloved hearts. Do not feel that Patience means standing still but rather standing poised in the *Tension of Light*.

> **Set your sights on the Ascension and you will not countenance impatience.**

The Arrow of Spirit quivers with anticipation of the next release. To reach its target, you must decide for yourself the goal and decide for yourself the mission that you will follow to achieve that goal. Above all, remember that Patience and Harmony work hand in hand with the All-Powerful Love of God.

> Do not feel that Patience means standing still but rather standing poised in the *Tension of Light*.

May the Comfort Flame of my Heart surround your Heart and bring you Peace this night in the stillness of the Great Silence of our meditation on God Patience.

I send to you my Love. I AM and I remain,

*The Maha Chohan*

*Beloved Mighty I AM Presence!*
*Charge and fill my feeling world*
*With your Great Ascended Master Patience!*

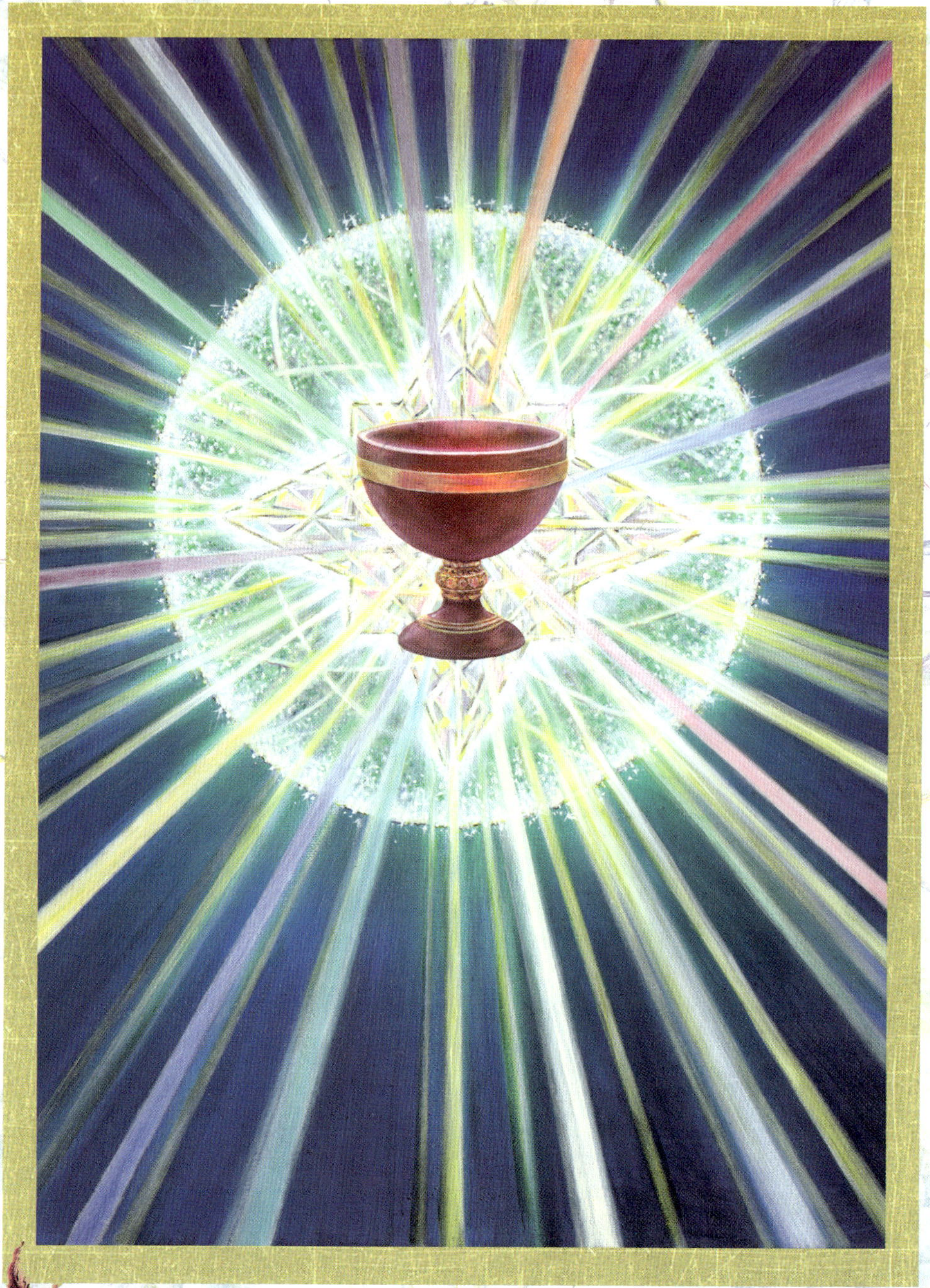

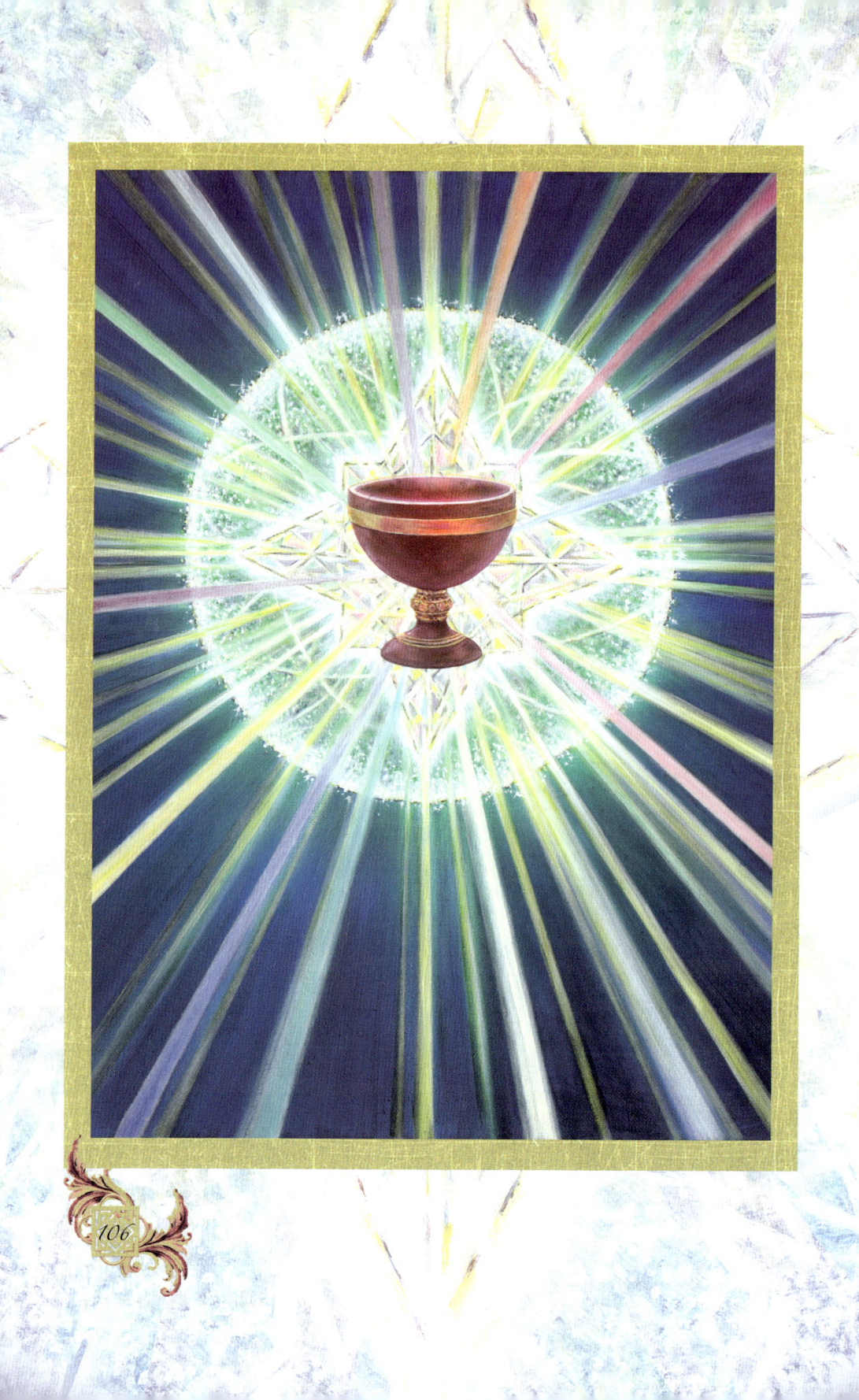

# Poise

Dear Light Bearers,

Let us consider those who for the first time begin to experience their world scintillating with Light, Fiery Essence, glowing with the excitement and Joy of a New Day and a new experience in Light! This Light is hard to hold. It must move. It must expand. And in the newness of the expansion of the Light there is naturally great excitement!

As that excitement moves within the vehicles of the novice, there are those who find themselves unable to control any number of activities of their bodies. Many times there is an expression of talking far too much, far too loud, not discriminating as to whom one is talking. There are times that this newfound Light will present itself in an agitation, an anxiousness, if you will.

Many will find that there is a tendency to want to run and accomplish everything before the end of the day that would otherwise take perhaps many weeks, months or years. All-in-all this excitement, if left unchecked, uncontrolled, will waste many of the precious ergs of energy of that precious Light.

So then how is one to control one's being when there is much to rejoice in, so much to be excited about, so much to accomplish? This brings us to the Mastery of Poise. Poise is bringing into your lifestream a sense of balance.

> Poise is bringing into your lifestream a sense of balance.

The answer lies in the necessity for each of the chakras, the energy centers of your vehicles, to be filled with this Light of which I speak. And as those energy centers are filled to capacity, the chakras will spin with a more than ordinary intensity, releasing a more than ordinary Fire! The key to the Mastery of that Fire is bringing each of those chakras into balance, allowing each to reach a heightened state of equilibrium of a stable Constancy in flow.

The greatest Mastery of the Light is when one can hold the position of balance, of equilibrium within their being, for it allows an alignment of the lower vehicles with the Liquid Light continually flowing from the Heart of the I AM Presence. This Power that is continually flowing must be held in reserve, waiting for the moment when it is to be released — not too soon and not too late. Every great general and warrior of the spirit has known that when they enter into battle this state of Poise will be tested. It will be necessary to not become anxious, impatient or angry prior to the very moment when there is the need for the release of the Arrow of Fire.

Many inner and outer worlds are turning constantly, and the balance between those worlds is held in check by the anchor point that is most present within the heart center of each system. And within that center point is a quiescence and a Fire that is holding still, not unlike the eye of a hurricane where all is moving around and away from that center, creating a vortex, while within the center all is quiet, still, steadfast. This is Poise. This is Mastery. This is not allowing your emotions, your ego, or fear to sway you. There is no force outside the Direction of your God Presence that is able to move one erg of energy before the appointed hour.

Poise takes Courage. Poise takes Fearlessness, Strength, Faith, Hope, and Charity. Every God Quality you can imagine is required to master Poise. Once you have studied and begun to master all other God Qualities, you will then be prepared to address Poise. You will find your posture will change. Your attitude will change. For an attitude in Poise carries the Grace, the Love, and the understanding of God Wisdom through Poise.

Practice, if you will, sitting quiet, not moving a muscle or blinking an eye. Allow just enough breath to carry the oxygen to the lungs. Hold that position and see

# Poise

how long you are able to sit without moving, without shifting your attention from your Presence, without flexing even a muscle. This is the requirement for the checking of the flow of Light into your being. For once you have mastered the understanding of what is required for Light, not only to enter the vehicles but to be released, you will then be entrusted with a greater responsibility of co-creating with that Light and becoming an adept.

> Your Presence is not wavering. It does not become anxious. It does not become excited.

These are part of the requirements, beloved ones, for each lifestream who is desirous of becoming one with their God Presence. Your Presence is not wavering. It does not become anxious. It does not become excited. It does not move too quickly or say things that are irrelevant or ill-timed.

As you continue on the Path, you will find that there will be days that you will desire to sit in the Silence. One observing from the outer might say this is a waste of time, that nothing is being accomplished. But if you are truly sitting in the Great Silence, contemplating the Heart of your God Presence, you are practicing the Mastery of Poise, you are mastering your desires. You are mastering the Light.

*Poise, beloved hearts, exudes Grace and Blessing. It projects Love and understanding.*

Poise allows for the Heart of your God Presence to be the one to engage with others. It allows the Christ Mind to contemplate each step, each interaction that is necessary for your lifestream. It allows for the Divine Self to be the one that moves into action in a timely manner, not preempting cycles and not missing cycles, but in a timely fashion.

If you do not master Poise you may not be able to be in a position of stillness in your inner being when it is time for your God Presence to call you Home. You may not hear that Inner Call, for you will be too preoccupied with trivial matters. You will have your own agenda. The outer ego will be in control.

Poise is elevating. You naturally rise in consciousness. You are able to truly experience Freedom when in a state of Poise. True Poise is true Harmony and true God Love in your world.

The balanced golden mean figure-eight flow of Light that begins and ends in the Great Central Sun, moving through your vehicles is in a constant state of movement, while still holding to a constant state of Poise. For you to interact and engage with this Light and flow with the cycles of the Sun there is a certain balance of Poise that is required.

## POISE

Practice in your daily activities holding your Harmony in a state of Poise when you would otherwise engage in an eruption of emotion that is less than harmonious. Sit in meditation and allow for a certain number of minutes each day to be engaged in Poise and Contemplation on your Presence. Balance your day so that you have the time necessary to accomplish these very meaningful exercises. Do not enter into those silent meditations anxious or rushed, for that would be most counterproductive to your state of Poise.

Poise is God Wisdom, for there truly is a necessity for an understanding of cycles, of timing. There comes Listening Grace and understanding of why and how and where. The engagement of one's energy into any activity requires understanding if true Poise is to be accomplished. And where there is lack of understanding, it requires Faith that your God Presence will alert you to the time to move and be in action.

> Poise is God Wisdom, for there truly is an understanding of cycles, of timing.

We could talk and discourse for many, many hours on all of the Divine Facets of Poise and how each will benefit your lifestream. Truly, the God Quality of Poise can bring the Fullness of God into all of your outer activities. You will then be able to hear the still, small

Voice. You will feel the nudge to go here or there. You will have the sense of correct timing and flow. You will have God Harmony in your world. And where there is God Harmony, there is God Love.

Give the call to your God Presence to, *"Charge and fill your feeling world with Ascended Master Poise!"* and you *will* win your Ascension when you have mastered this God Quality and all that it portends.

I leave you in the Stillness of Poise.

*The Maha Chohan*

*Beloved Mighty I AM Presence!
Charge and fill my feeling world
With your Great Ascended Master Poise!*

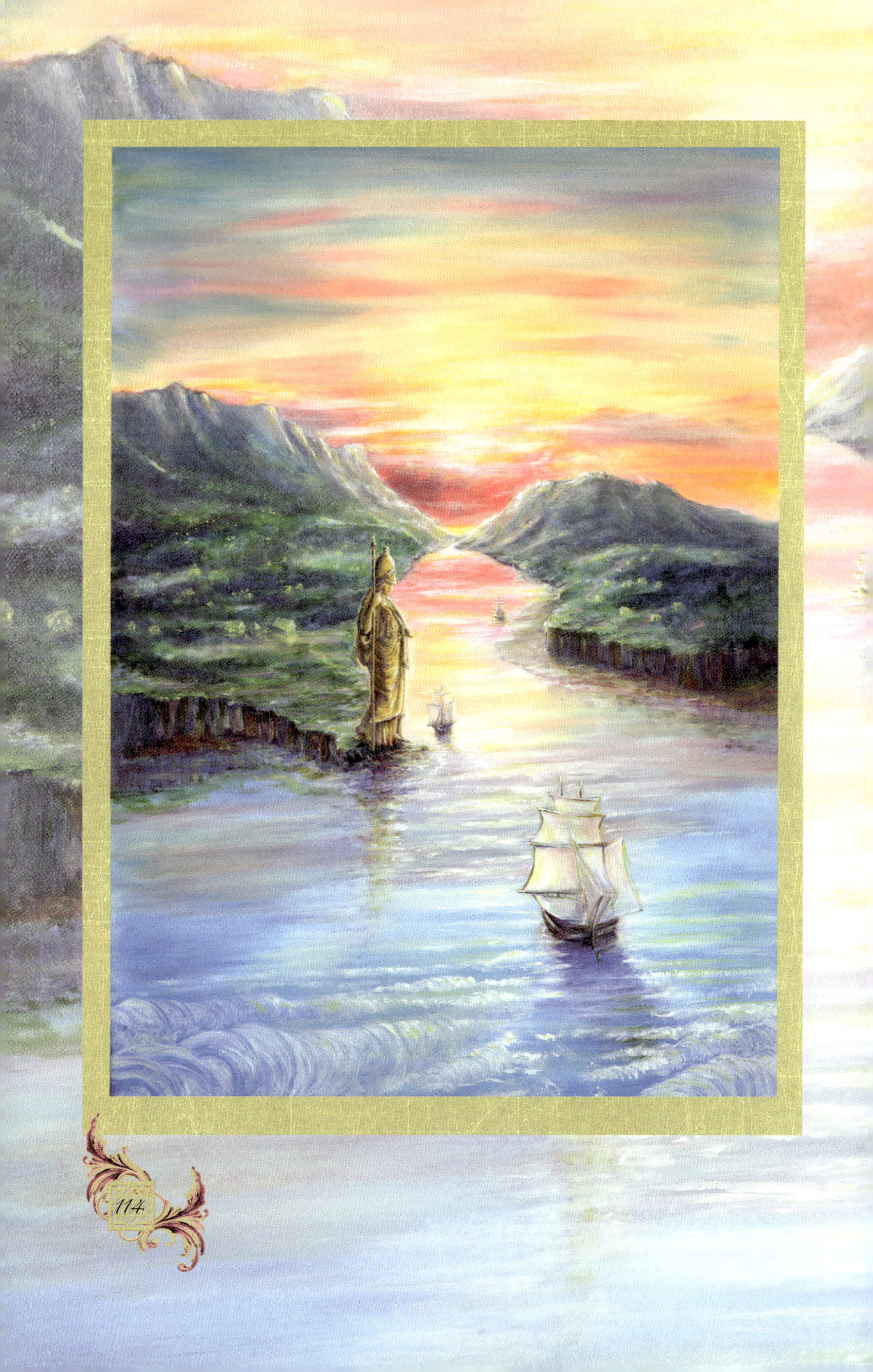

# Humility

My Dear Hearts,

As you continue to study the *Ruby Chalice* of my Heart and to go within the Chalice of your own Heart to discover who you are, I should like to share with you the understanding of the Essence of Reality of your God Presence and the unreality of the human ego.

For many, from the earliest time of childhood, there is only the recollection of the growing human ego and the process of making decisions based on worldly facts and limitations as imposed from without by all of those experiences you have been exposed to. If you are fortunate, there was within you the inner connection with your Holy Christ Presence at a very young age that was encouraged and allowed to expand and to become the strengthening rod by which you co-measure all other facts and disciplines imposed.

## Humility

As you continued to grow up and learn the ways of the world, even where there was the initial tie with your Christ Presence at early ages, you began to move away from its intrinsic values that had been so very much a part of your beginning. It was not that those engagements in the world were so terribly wrong, but were they for you? Were they the Garments that you were called upon by your own God Presence to wear?

So in the course of learning how to make wise decisions and what voices to hear and adhere to, you began to realize that you, as an individual, with a heart, with a voice, with a will to do, could begin to engage in forms of creating — could take action, could speak, and you could create. Many of your creations were satisfying to your lifestream.

You elected to continue to pursue that same course. And when those around you would congratulate you and reward you with earthly treasures, you determined that you were on the right course of action and you became self-assured that this was the path for you.

And so, imperceptibly with the passing of the years, the still small Voice of the Heart of your own Holy Christ Presence was relegated somewhere into the very far background awareness of your life's experiences. For you had learned to attend to the voice of the mind, to respond to the desires of the flesh, and to hold in your vision accomplishments prized by the world.

# HUMILITY

This became your suit of armor, allowing you to move about, here and there, holding your head high with the self-assurance that you had accomplished great things. You had brought forth manifest creations from your own works. And yes, all around you were acclaiming your victory.

With your eye upon the future, you envisioned yourself in all manner of creative activity along the same lines and with greater acclaim. Did you ever consider what enabled your opportunity to create? Where ultimately did the Light and Energy come from to perform the works that you so graciously with ease were taking credit for? The Light and Energy came from your God Presence.

> The Light and Energy came from your God Presence.

Those who have been students of the Inner Teachings from the Ascended Masters have been reminded time and again of the greater benefit and Greater Works that come forth from the Light of their own God Presence, when it is allowed to imbue their every effort. The Light itself is impersonal as it comes through the Crystal Cord and enters into the chakras. What you do with that Light, however, is wholly another story.

But where did the Good Works originate from? Were they of the mind? Were they of the hands? And

## Humility

what propelled the mind and what guided the hands, if not the Light? And when that Light came forth was there the understanding of the responsibility for its wise use?

So many times from your very earliest childhood, you have assumed that you personally have done a great work. With chest puffed high, shoulders drawn back, and head raised, you have taken all the credit. And even when you have shyly, with false humility, denied the acclaim, beneath all your protestations you secretly congratulated yourself on your accomplishments.

Consider for a moment: Was it the understanding with your Holy Christ Presence fully engaged that you elected to bring forth the creation and your good works? Was it in ignorance to the Law? Were you in fact engaged with your Holy Christ Presence and knew not? Or, have you sincerely desired to give the glory and acclaim to the Heart of God, your own God Presence, where all has come from of any worth or great value?

Many do not realize the false humility that they project, patting themselves on the back and giving their outer self all of the glory, when in reality the Light comes forth from your own God Presence into the Heart. You receive, daily, the Light of God, and this is the Light with which you take your breath, beat your heart, move your hands, and think your thoughts.

Recognize that the outer expression of your God Presence is the body temple you wear, and allow for the body temple, that vehicle of physical expression of your God Presence, to be the extension, the hands and feet in the service of your Presence to do the Works that are desired by your God Presence in this world of form. All your vehicles are connected through the Heart. Your God Presence, your Holy Christ Presence, and your body temple each resonate with the same Heart. Therefore, know who you are!

> *When there is the correct understanding of creation and how the Light of God performs the Perfect Works through you, there cannot be anything in your world but Divine Humility.*

For you understand that you have only been the vehicle, that the Directing Intelligence was the part of life of you that is God.

And thus your Holy Christ Presence stands patiently waiting for every opportunity to engage in your life to bring you the great Wisdom of your own God Presence and the Directing Intelligence to move your lifestream into all of the areas of accomplishment and great lessons to be learned that are the Desire of your God Presence. Absent the Holy Christ Presence, one most certainly can take credit for their accomplishments, but in reality, they are only the vanity of mortal accomplishments of yet another round of incarnation while passing through these octaves of the physical plane, spawning ever more barren human miscreations.

## Humility

Hopefully, following the transition into devachan, there is an opportunity to continue to learn and to practice creating what is beautiful and fulfilling those Divine Aspirations left unfulfilled so that when you come into incarnation once again, there is another opportunity for you to listen for the Inner Voice of your Holy Christ Presence and to receive its guidance to keep you on track.

Therefore, know full well that it is not the human ego that has accomplished any great work at all, rather it is the Light and the talents of your own God Presence. You could say that It, the Mighty I AM Presence, is who you truly are. And, in fact, that is exactly who you are in action fulfilling the Will of God.

> …it is not the human ego that has accomplished any great work at all, rather it is the Light and the talents of your own God Presence…

But when there is not that conscious recognition and one continues to deny the existence of the Holy Christ Self and God Presence and elects to do all from their own self will, know full well that such accomplishments and the fruit will not carry the High Vibration for the benefit either to your life or any other part of life that was expected by your own God Presence of your lifestream. You may accomplish things. You may create things. But they will not be the Creations of God.

# HUMILITY

The co-creative process with your God Presence engaged and directing the outcome will give you the opportunity to give the credit where credit is truly due. And that credit is to your own Divine Self. Any time you may be tempted to give yourself credit for an accomplishment, consider instantly the Light of your God Presence. Look to the eyes of your own God Presence in Honor and Gratitude.

*Humility in the Divine Essence of Love and Gratitude to God is the mark and measure of the true disciple on the Path.*

*The Maha Chohan*

*Beloved Mighty I AM Presence!
Charge and fill my feeling world
With your Great Ascended Master Humility!*

122

# Courage

My Dear Student of the Light,

I come to you in the Fullness of the Flame of Courage. Courage that each and every Son and Daughter of God must experience, exemplify, and be fortified with in order to realize the full expansion of the Light of the Threefold Flame of the Heart.

Courage begins when the newborn infant takes its first breath of air upon entering earth's atmosphere. It takes Courage to draw that breath, knowing it marks the beginning of a new lifelong cycle. The next major feat of Courage is taking the first step. Watching a child take their first step, you may remember how important it is to keep their balance and their equilibrium, how they must concentrate on their direction and their goal in order to maintain the necessary alignment. Believe it or not, a child considers all these things. Oh, to behold such determination of the Heart to take that first step, determination so great it outweighs all possibilities of failure.

Throughout your lifetime you encounter many opportunities to exemplify Courage. For many, getting up in the morning and starting a new day takes courage. But this courage is not born through the Fires of the Purity of the Heart for the Love of Life. This is an ill-fated courage born of fear. The roar of the lion may scare away many, but it is not true Courage that roars.

*Courage is born of the Heart through Wisdom's Flame.*

Blessed one, here is your formula for true Courage. Purity of Heart cradles the determination of Wisdom's Flame, and the Will of God exemplifies Patience, holding fast to the moment, while never losing contact with the pure understanding of the Christ Mind — then Courage is born.

It is easy to be Fearless when one is surrounded by others of a courageous nature and where you have the ability to be protected by their shield. But the true warrior on the Path can stand alone in his own Light, in the Fullness of the Flame of his own Courage, and move forward as an Adept.

True Courage knows only the Light of God, knows only the Victorious beginning and ending of the battle. The real Strength to evoke Courage requires the Strength to hold true to your Heart. Those who waver, those who doubt or question the prompting of their

Heart, open the door to fear. Fear brings trembling and a crumbling of the very foundation of Courage.

Many of the great conquerors of old were known for their Courage. They were not known for fierceness but for their unrelenting determination for the Love of God in the Holy Cause of Freedom. Freedom is born of the invincible Flame of the Heart. Those who would follow choose not the weak, the meek or the mild. They choose those who radiate Courage, Wisdom, genuine understanding, and that Divine Compassion born of the true Love of the Heart.

> Freedom is born of the invincible Flame of the Heart.

The Ascended Masters are looking for such leaders — leaders who will make the Cause of the Flame of Freedom their life's work. The Brotherhood of Light is on the march bearing the Torch of Freedom's Flame to a waiting world! A prerequisite for our Torch Bearers is Courage. For Courage is just one step ahead of Freedom, beloved one. In every age there is always a dividing of the way. Those few who elect to move forward into the Light of their own Ascension shall blaze a Path for the many who follow. These stalwart ones are they who have mastered the art of Courage.

## Courage

> Under his watchful gaze, you are never permitted any trial where you cannot emerge Victorious.

Those Torch Bearers determined to gain their Eternal Freedom can expect continual testing from childhood on. This is but to strengthen you, for the striving becomes greater, the tests harder, more painful and enduring, as you approach closer to your final Victory.

The Great Initiator, Lord Maitreya, is always on the alert for such as these. Under his watchful gaze, you are never permitted any trial where you cannot emerge Victorious. Then shall not the Fires of your Heart burn more brightly with the Will of God in Courage?

I trust that the next time you see a child who is but a toddler, you will look closely into the eyes of that child and see there the God Determination to be Victorious. You cannot be Victorious, beloved one, without Courage, and to have Courage you must have Strength. For Courage lives in the strong rarefied atmosphere of the pure Heart. Your spiritual armor must be strengthened by the Will of God, by Wisdom's Flame, and the pure Love of the Heart.

Regardless of the onslaught of opposition, why should you be fearful or suffer doubt or trepidation about moving forward with any worthwhile task when you know that you have the Fullness of the Light of God as your shield? Fear moves in only when there is a breach in your shield, when some part of your armor has been neglected. Then you feel a shaking within your members.

This should be an immediate sign to you, beloved one, to gird up your loins. You must not go into battle unprotected. There are those foolish enough to think they can do all, be all, win all through their own might and mien. This is a foolish heart indeed. For only as you stand in the Light and attunement of your I AM Presence are you fully protected.

Too many times when faced with the greatest battles on our doorstep, we forget to listen. We become so confused and engrossed in the immediacy of the battle that we forget the still small Voice of God speaking within and giving us Divine Direction. It takes ultimate Courage to be still and listen.

Anyone can clash and clank their armor, but it takes Strength and ultimate Courage to have the Patience to know when to hold fast, when to hold steady in the Light, when to listen till the Direction is firm and clear, and then to move forward in the full conviction that you are already Victorious in the Light.

I once gave instruction regarding the critical importance of forging and sustaining this *Thread of Contact* even amidst the most dire outer

# COURAGE

world circumstances. I wish that you should study it directly, for it carries my full conviction regarding the importance of remaining always enfolded in the calm, poised, supremely confident Radiance and Peace of your own Holy Christ Presence.

It also takes Courage to deal with illnesses and pain in your physical body. When one is faced with grave illnesses that are outpicturing in the physical body, one must muster up the Courage to honestly address that pain, to touch it, and if necessary to learn the lessons surrounding its cause. Whether or not your conscious mind makes the connection, rest assured that inwardly you will know the reason why. Then call on the Law of Forgiveness for yourself, release the record and memory, and allow for its full transmutation. I afford you my Comfort Flame immediately upon contact with that pain.

> Beloved one, in those hours of your personal trial, I, the Maha Chohan, will be there with my Comfort Flame.

This process is not easy. But oftentimes it is a necessary part of dealing with the intense record and of being able to put it into the Violet Flame, lest you carry that karmic inclination over into succeeding embodiments and have a reoccurrence. Beloved one, in those hours of your personal trial, I, the Maha Chohan, will be there with my Comfort Flame, I promise you.

## Courage

Have you not wondered why many mothers giving birth to a child continue to have more children and more children, even though the pain of giving birth is so great? It is because the moment the child is born and the Holy Spirit descends there is such a Comfort released to the mother that the full Joy of the birth of the child far outweighs any traces of the memory of pain. Oh, there are those who will jest and talk about their discomforts, but in their hearts they know the Fullness of the Joy they have experienced. For many mothers it is the greatest opportunity in their entire lifetime to render a Divine Service and thereby to experience the Fullness of the Light of God.

> I will salute you as you come home to claim your Robes of Valor.

My Comfort Flame of the Holy Spirit is available to every one of God's children. All anyone need do is ask and they will receive. The next time you find yourself faced with having to be Courageous, remember my words. Put on your armor. Assess the situation. Then call for the Fullness of the release of the Will of God into the situation. Stand tall. Wear the Mantle of your own I AM Presence proudly, knowing you will be Victorious. And I will salute you as you come home to claim your Robes of Valor.

# Courage

I AM the Maha Chohan, and I stand for your Courage. I may not hold your hand going into battle lest I take away part of your opportunity, but I can stand behind you. And I shall go before you if you but remember to claim the Fullness of your God Identity. I leave you now with my promised instruction on sustaining the *Thread of Contact* with your God Self.

> ... *Then will come a calm such as comes in a tropical country after the heavy rain, when Nature works so swiftly that one may see her action. Such a calm will come to the harassed spirit. And in the deep Silence the mysterious event will occur which will prove that the Way has been found. Call it by what name you will, it is the Voice that speaks where there is none to speak — it is a Messenger that comes, a Messenger without form or substance; it is the flower of the soul that has opened. It cannot be described by any metaphor. But it can be felt after, looked for, and desired, even amid the raging of the storm. The Silence may last a moment of time or it may last a thousand years. But it will end. Yet you will carry its Strength with you. Again and again the battle must be fought and won. It is only for an interval that Nature can be still.*
>
> *Out of the Silence that is Peace a resonant Voice shall arise. And this Voice will say, "It is not well; thou*

hast reaped, now thou must sow." And knowing this Voice to be the Silence itself, thou wilt obey. Thou who art now a Disciple, able to stand, able to hear, able to see, able to speak, who hast conquered desire and attained to Self-knowledge, who hast seen thy soul in its bloom and recognized it, and heard the Voice of the Silence, go thou to the Hall of Learning and read what is written there for thee.

> Stand aside in the coming battle, and though thou fightest, be not the Warrior.

> Look for the Warrior and let Him fight in thee.

> Take his orders for battle and obey them.

> Obey Him not as though He were a general, but as though He were Thyself, and his spoken Words were the utterance of thy secret desires; for He is Thyself, yet infinitely wiser and stronger than thyself. Look for Him, else in the fervor and hurry of the fight thou mayest pass Him; and He will not know thee unless thou knowest Him. If thy cry meet His listening ear, then will He fight in thee and fill the dull void within. And if this is so, then canst thou go through the fight cool and unwearied, standing aside and letting Him battle for thee. Then it will be impossible for thee to strike one blow amiss. But if thou look not for Him, if thou pass Him by, then there is no safeguard for thee.

## Courage

*Thy brain will reel, thy heart grow uncertain, and in the dust of the battlefield thy sight and senses will fail, and thou wilt not know thy friends from thine enemies...*

*... You can stand upright now, firm as a rock amid the turmoil, cool and awakened, obeying the Warrior who is thy Self and thy King. Unconcerned in the battle save to do his bidding, having no longer any care as to the result of the battle, for one thing only is important, that the Warrior shall win, and you know He is incapable of defeat...* [1]

My Love I send with you into the battle.

### The Maha Chohan

**Beloved Mighty I AM Presence!**
**Charge and fill my feeling world**
**With your Great Ascended Master Courage!**

---

[1] Collins, Mabel, *Light on the Path*, George Redway, London, 1888

Courage

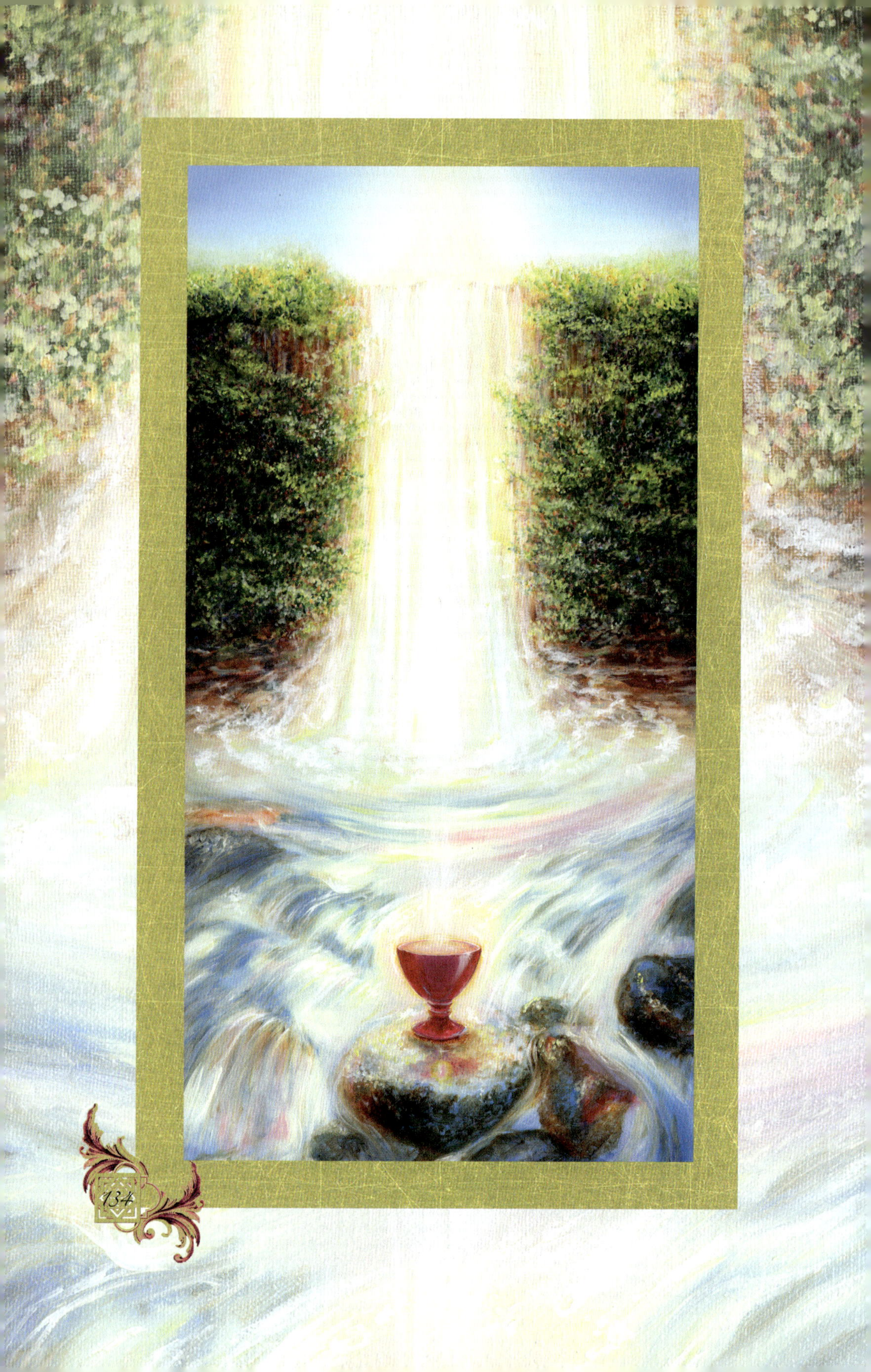

# Strength

My Beloved Students of the Light,

I charge and fill your feeling world with Ascended Master Strength! Strength that you can call upon at any hour of the day! The Brotherhood stands with you. We are ready to do battle, ready to come forth with the Stronghold of our Strength, of that overpowering Ascended Master Radiation which you need to meet and defeat the world's chaos.

Much Courage can be summoned, along with Determination and Will, but what if there is not sufficient Strength for the battle? Your personal Strength, beloved ones, stands with that of the Entire Brotherhood. We are ready to move forward with you, to give you the understanding, the guidance, and the Teachings you need and to buoy you up when you feel that you cannot move forward another step.

STRENGTH

True Strength, beloved ones, is a singular commodity. Today especially, many think it has to do with muscles, with the strength of mere flesh and blood. I tell you nay. *Ascended Master Strength is the Fortitude of the Light!* Contact with that Light, sustained firmly through your God Will and God Determination, is the true measure of your Strength. Beloved ones, the constantly flowing stream of Liquid Light from your own Mighty I AM Presence is the supreme nourishment that your body needs for Strength. It can repair even the physical chalice where it is broken.

If ever there is a weakness in your forcefield, if ever you allow the breakdown of the physical temple, those astral forces that would not like you to accomplish your Mission move into action. They say "Aha! She is in a weakened state. Now we can have our way." They look for that unguarded moment when you neglect your prayer or decree momentum and thus allow the flow of Light from your Presence to diminish. The Light is your ultimate protection! Therefore, it is absolutely necessary for you to maintain your personal forcefield as a Stronghold of Strength through your decrees.

> **Ascended Master Strength is the Fortitude of the Light!**

You ask, "How do I keep on keeping on in the face of such worldly pressures?" It is very simple, beloved ones.

Where your thoughts are, there your energy goes. Do you understand? If your thoughts are scattered throughout the chaos and confusion of the battle, you will not forge the necessary Divine Contact to draw support from your Source.

> It takes summoning all the Strength within you to hold fast to the Heights of God Consciousness…

You cannot allow such chaos or confusion to enter into your personal world. You cannot permit your thoughts to waver from the Heart of your own I AM Presence. If you have difficulty accepting that the Stronghold of your Electronic Body is ever close and that it is a very real and immediate part of your world, then put your thought and attention on one of the Ascended Masters. Put your hand in their hand. Meditate on their Heart.

Do not be alarmed when I remind you that there is indeed opposition pitted against you individually and collectively to keep you from your Victory, from winning your Ascension. The only way to have the full Strength to battle this opposition is to maintain your unbroken contact with the Light.

Sustaining this attunement is not always easy. It takes summoning all the Strength within you to hold fast to the Heights of God Consciousness, to make your calls, and then to accept those returning Waves of Light from your Presence to bear you forward to Victory.

## Strength

Beloved ones, I AM not without Compassion. I know many of you have emotional scars in your past that can easily produce fear and trepidation in your world. And many times you feel you have not the Strength for yet one more battle. This is only a state of mind. Or to be more precise — a state of your mental body.

Too much importance cannot be placed on understanding the critical importance of maintaining the *quality* of *all* your thoughts as the foundation to mastering your mind. My Son, El Morya, speaks much on this subject. You would do well to study his teaching on thought.

Many times when a feeling of inertia or fear of lack enters your world for whatever reason, you must go immediately into your Heart.

### *The Heart is the true barometer and connecting point with Higher Octaves.*

Allow the flow of your attention to carry you into the Heart, into the Secret Chamber, and there to make the full connection with the Light of your own God Identity. Once you have achieved this, remain in this attunement as long as necessary to infuse your world with the God Determination to move forward, knowing you are protected with the Shield of Light, the Shield of your Presence.

I would like to speak of another form of the desecration of your lifestream that may not be readily apparent to you but nevertheless causes great fatigue in your world.

Oftentimes we overlook the small offenses against the Holy Spirit, thinking that only the great battles merit the full intensity of our efforts towards self-mastery. Beloved ones, I'm referring to the minor irritations that you indulge yourselves in.

Something so simple and apparently insignificant is easily overlooked, but if you do not arrest these irritations as they present themselves and immediately introduce Harmony and Peace back into your world, you will find that in the crucial hour when your greatest Strength is needed, your reserves of Light will have been depleted. The precious Life of your God Presence, intended to be accumulated and held in reserve in your emotional body, will instead have been lost, and you will find yourself wanting.

Throughout your day, this or that little pinpoint of irritation enters in, each one puncturing your aura and draining away its thimbleful of Light. The forces of opposition know only too well the ultimate consequence to your lifestream and take great delight when they succeed in catching you off guard.

The sooner you realize that "Eternal Vigilance" is *a must* for disciples of the Ascended Masters, the sooner you will have done with irritation and any number of other lamentable traits unworthy of your grand and glorious God Self! Such Vigilance requires maintaining a certain degree of spiritual tension, which simply means training your attention to hold fast to the Light even midst the most trying circumstances.

## Strength

When once you have forged the conscious connection with the Light of your own Holy Christ Presence and Beloved I AM Presence, all of Heaven stands at your beck and call. Rest in the confidence that Peace, Harmony, and the release of Ascended Master Light will continue to flood your world, knowing that you can produce lasting results for good, knowing that you can be that masterful Presence whom you choose to be.

***Standing in this Light, you will feel the full measure of Courage and Strength of which I speak.***

You must also guard against certain other outer conditions that would knowingly or unknowingly drain your energy. Oftentimes a blessed one close to you has come to live entirely on your externalized efforts and your Life Currents to the exclusion of their own. Truly they know not what they do. But you must recognize it and deal with it in a harmonious manner, demanding Divine Order and Divine Justice to reorder the circumstances of your life, setting you free of all unlawful associations or dependencies.

Finally — if you are truly serious about your Path — you must not suffer associations with any individual who practices abuse of any kind, physical, emotional or verbal. Mere words, so called, are enough to bring fatigue when there is anger or belittlement charged into them. When that fatigue sets in, you do not always recognize why you are tired, or why you simply wish to escape.

# STRENGTH

Dear ones! Again I say, "Go into the Heart." Your Heart is the greatest barometer for detecting and identifying whatever form of discordant energy that might assail you. The feeling world does not always tell you. The mental world certainly does not tell you. But the Heart will. Listen to the Heart. Once having attuned with the Heart, be courageous enough to recognize these conditions for what they are, then draw forth the Light through your Heart to dissolve the discord.

> Allow Us to help you meet every challenge on your pathway back to the Heart of God.

I, the Maha Chohan, breathe forth into your world now the Breath of Life, together with that magnificent Stream of qualified Sacred Fire known to Us at Inner Levels as the *Entire Spirit of the Brotherhood of Light!* Allow Us to help you meet every challenge on your pathway back to the Heart of God. Nothing brings Us more Joy than to be of assistance to each and every one of you.

I bid you good day in the full Strength and Light of my Heart.

*The Maha Chohan*

**Beloved Mighty I AM Presence!**
**Charge and fill my feeling world**
**With your Great Ascended Master Strength!**

142

# Fearlessness

Fear not for behold I bring you good tidings of Great Joy!

This day Beloved Gabriel and his Band of Angels are winging their way to your side to stand in the Service of your God Self and teach you Fearlessness. Accept their ministrations and allow your Heart to open wide and project the Fullness of Courage and Strength garnered within the Secret Chamber of the Heart.

Many aspirants on the Path have not felt equipped with the necessary tools with which to stand, face, and conquer victoriously all that assails them. Therefore, through doubts, fears, and records of questioning, these lifestreams have stepped back in retreat instead of stepping forward with a Heart full of Faith and the fervor of a pure intent which would carry them to their Victory.

Beloved ones, fear is not always acquired within the present lifetime. Many records of past transgressions — the pains, hurts, and discouragements that you have experienced in other lifetimes — have been carried forward as a karmic weight pressing down on your Heart. There they block the opening of the petals of the Heart Chakra. They block the witness of the Holy Spirit which would otherwise produce genuine Comfort and trust that all is truly well within your being.

Beloved ones, that instinctive trust in God's Power to answer your every need is a necessary ingredient to the release of the Fullness of Fearlessness Flame. You cannot afford to entertain anything less than the sense of absolute security and complete well-being in God if you hope to stand courageously in Fearlessness Flame.

In this physical world the unimpeded flow of the Currents of Light through your world is the veritable shield of your being! Wherever any condition is allowed to interrupt that flow, you will sense a quivering in your members. You will certainly experience less than the Fullness of the Ray of your own God Presence that is to nurture each of your chakras.

Beloved ones, fear only exists where there is an insufficiency of Light, and by that I mean the unmitigated intensity of the Light of your own I AM Presence or that of one of the Ascended Masters. When you achieve the full action of this Flame — the momentum of Fearlessness which you release from your Heart out into your world — you will have the Courage to stand and meet all life's challenges at the appointed hour.

But if that Heart is weighted down in records of discouragement, anger, doubt, resentment or irritation — Fearlessness cannot be summoned from the Heart and complete its Perfect Work. Instead the fear acts like an unbalanced weight attached to the sleek Arrow of Light causing it to swerve off course and miss the intended mark.

Again I ask that you consider how a child approaches new opportunities. Have you noticed the daring fortitude of most children? Whenever something new and daunting looms before them, they do not worry about all that might go wrong or assail them. They simply move forward. They have not yet absorbed the world's anxieties or skepticism, but step forward instinctively, moving with the speed of Light, with their eye focused on the goal and advancing boldly into the next cycle of their life. Such advances mark the beginning of a child's education in working with the Sacred Fire.

> Fearlessness Flame is at the core of the Fire that will carry you to your Ascension.

Fearlessness Flame is at the core of the Fire that will carry you to your Ascension. If you dally, if you hesitate, you will not have the opportunity to accomplish all that you have aspired to within this lifetime. You must establish

## Fearlessness

a rhythmic flow, a Constancy of forward movement and momentum within your being for the Ascension Currents to manifest the Fullness of all that you desire.

To wholeheartedly seek after God with all your might takes much Courage indeed. It has come to my attention that many students do not take such monumental life changing steps out of the fear that their world will change in ways beyond their control, sensing that they will neither think nor act in the old familiar fashion. This fear is such a travesty for an Ascended Master to behold.

For how is the planet Earth to move forward into a Golden Age when there is such fear and trembling and trepidation even on the part of those who know they are called to the Path? Certainly there is a fear of loss, but how could you actually lose something that was never yours to begin with? For it was never Real. How can you attain to God Reality and Truth without the loss of the maya and illusion which surround you?

> If you are to enter into a life filled with our Light, there must be a *Fearless* letting go of all that is not Real!

Whatever paltry trophies of past human identity you have chosen to clutch fast around yourself, they are but "familiars" of times past, of embodiments long gone by. If you are to enter into a life filled with our Light, there must be a *Fearless* letting go of all that is not Real!

# FEARLESSNESS

> You must keep your gaze steadfast upon the Light.

Many of you have no idea of the many transgressions against the Light committed in this and previous embodiments which yet remain within the folds of your emotional body and in the depths of the astral plane. Beloved hearts, if you are in earnest about entering into the Octaves of Light, it is necessary for your four lower bodies to be filled with Ascended Master Light — which Light alone can bear you upward into the Ascension!

Before this Initiation can be your own experience, you must be able to traverse the abyss of the astral plane. Due to past transgressions which remain as accumulated darkness within the astral plane, there often remains an irrational fear of traversing that abyss. To become the Fullness of the Light, you must understand that the Holy Angels are in attendance upon your lifestream daily to help you traverse this otherwise impassable gulf separating you from the Higher Octaves and the Retreats of the Masters.

As you sleep at night there is the opportunity for you to enter into higher education in the Realms of Light. But if you do not put your attention and your gaze upon this goal, there will not be the impetus of Will within you to stand in Fearlessness and take that step, that giant leap across the abyss. You cannot look back, you most

# Fearlessness

certainly cannot look down. You must keep your gaze steadfast upon the Light.

I, the Maha Chohan, stand ready to wrap you in my Comfort Flame and to allow you the opportunity of my Peace and Strength as a foundation for the full release of the Power of your God Self. When you stand in this place of Divine Authority, there is no concern for any mortal danger, no concern of what may assail you. *For only Light and Light alone is Victor!*

> For only Light and Light alone is Victor!

Yes, beloved hearts, you will do battle, but it will not be a struggle as an onslaught of danger but as the opportunity of forging greater Light and Life into your being through testing and Initiation. This is opportunity! It is a labor of working with the Light. As you outpicture greater Light within you, there will be a greater opportunity for selfless service, self-sacrifice, and surrender on behalf of the greater good of your Brothers and Sisters of Light.

But if you are not bold enough to take that first step, if there is not a Ray of Fearlessness that overcomes the terminal disease of hesitation, who will take your place? Will someone of equal or greater talents step forward to serve out the term of your own neglected Mission?

It is one thing to wrestle with the bag and baggage of your own karmic burden as you engage in Cosmic Service, but it is another to have that same human substance color and shape and deform and perhaps abort your destined Mission for an entire embodiment! Therefore, the intent of your Heart must be pure, if your gift of Service is to be pure and if that gift is to carry the magnitude of the Light and Truth of your God Presence acting through you.

Without giving any power to appearances, contemplate for a moment your greatest fear. What would that be? How would it look? When would it appear? Then apply Cosmic Law to each aspect of your fear. Is your fear based on immediate considerations or hypothetical possibilities? Is your fear based in Reality? I think not, beloved hearts! For *only* the Light of God is REAL! The grim masks of illusion and maya would intimidate you if you let them, causing you for the moment to lose sight of your Wonderful, Powerful, and Almighty Presence.

But, beloved ones, those masks are merely projected from your own untransmuted substance. They are abject refugees of your private underworld that would pass directly into the Flame of Transmutation were it not for the fear they manage to engender in you. In reality they are nothing more than an unhappy part of your past that does not want to go into the Flame. Any dalliance on your part about releasing your hold on this substance produces a sense of struggle and the so-called "battle" of Light and darkness instead of the instantaneous lopsided

Victory of Light over darkness! Such dalliances leave room for a cold fear of unnamed loss and change to deter your resolve and leave you searching about for all manner of excuses to postpone that day of change.

I must tell you a cosmic joke, for the joke will be upon you, beloved ones! *That change will come whether you choose the hour or not!* So why prolong the process? Why drag and kick and scream all the way to the Sacred Fire when you could stand, face, and conquer by the Light of the Central Sun and become the Son of God right where you are?

### *Let go of all that is not Real and put on the Garment of your own Christ Identity!*

This Mantle of the Christ is not painful, it will not deceive you, it will not disturb you, or lead you into harm's way. It will nourish you, protect you, guide and guard you, and most of all, love you.

What is there to be feared from throwing yourself without reservation into the Path? You have all of Heaven standing, waiting to give you the guidance and help to reach your goals. Do not hesitate another day to take this step. Do not hesitate to run and greet the Light of each new day, ready to release into your world the use of Fearlessness Flame.

# Fearlessness

> You have all of Heaven standing, waiting to give you the guidance and help to reach your goals.

I do not advocate an attitude of rushing in "where Angels fear to tread," but you are able to move forward knowing that you have the Light of God within your Heart enabling you to become all that your God Presence is already at Inner Levels. If you dally, you may never know, at least in this lifetime, all that you can become, all that you can do. Why you might even be able to make your Ascension!

I extend my Hand to meet yours as you demonstrate the Faith and trust in this formula of single-minded, wholehearted devotion to your Divine Path. Until we meet on that Path, I will hold the Flame for you in my Heart and extend Fearlessness Flame for your Victory!

Devotedly I AM,

*The Maha Chohan*

*Beloved Mighty I AM Presence!*
*Charge and fill my feeling world*
*With your Great Ascended Master Fearlessness!*

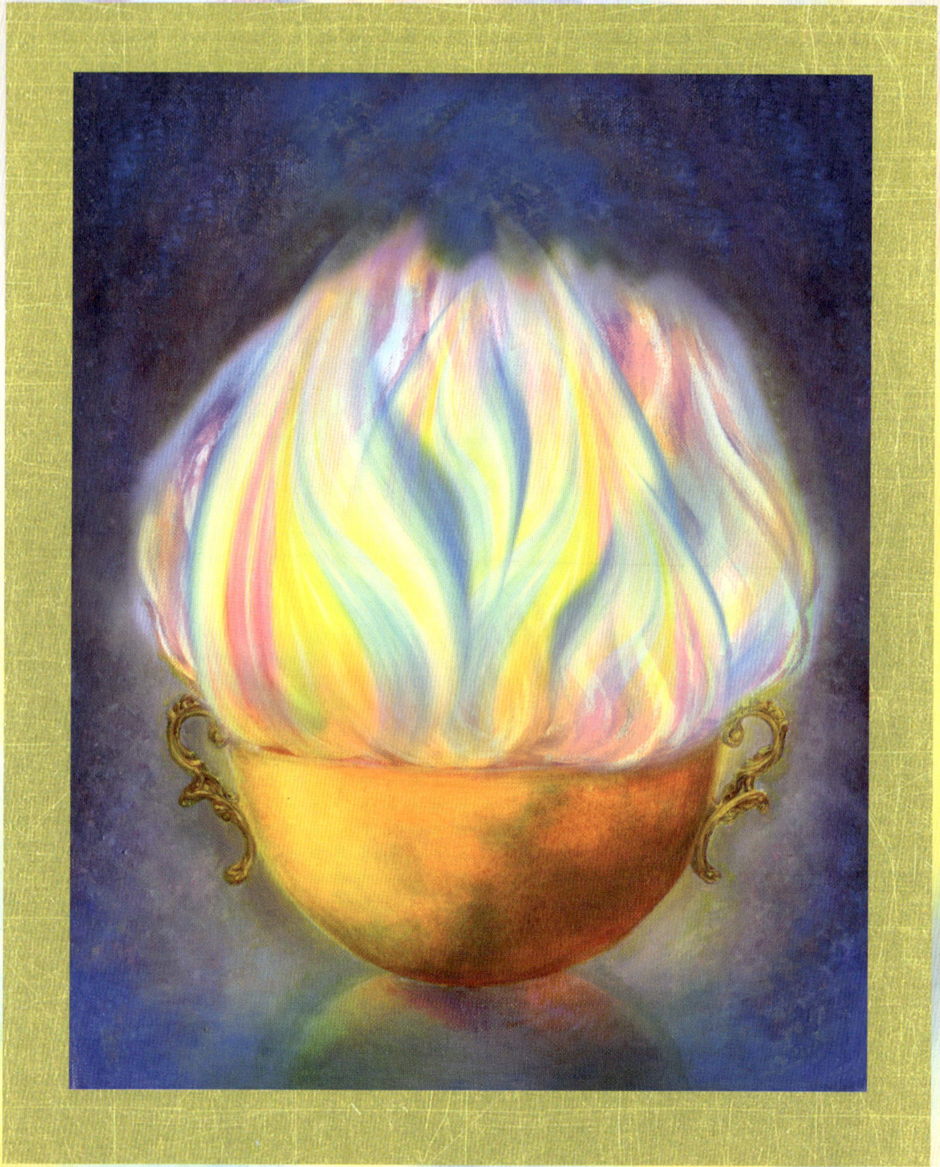

# Fire

**D**ear Hearts,

We take up the study of Fire. You hear this term used much in our instruction. You have heard of the Fires of the Holy Spirit, the Fires of the Heart, the Kundalini Fires, and the Flame of the Ascension. Have you stopped to imagine how much of your world is infused with Fire? Verily, the firing of the Electrons of Light in your body keep you moving forward toward the magnet of the Great Central Sun, your Cosmic Home of Light.

This is Sacred Fire that will consume all out of alignment with the Vibration of the God Quality. As the intense action of Fire moves through the records of past and present embodiments, there is an opportunity for greater and greater purification. When there is purification, there is wholeness. When there is wholeness, there is the Christ Consciousness. And in the Light of the Christ Consciousness you abide in the full Flame of your own I AM Presence.

There are many guideposts leading you to this ultimate opportunity. First and foremost, you must realize you already possess three Flames — three God Flames acting as one and abiding upon your Heart — God Illumination, God Will, and God Love. They are the living, tangible Presence of the Great God Flame, nurtured by your own Holy Christ Presence and I AM Presence, breathed on by the breath of the Holy Spirit and sustained by that Fire so you might have all you require lifetime after lifetime. This Threefold Flame is the Light that illumines your pathway Home. Oh yes, there are artificial lights which confuse and distract, but this Light, the Light of your own Heart Flame, can always be trusted.

I speak now of the Light of the chakras and of the Kundalini Fires that come forth, rising up when you least expect the awakening. Beloved ones, this is a Fire not to be toyed with. Regard its arrival seriously. In your world you have learned to treat electricity in its many outward forms with great respect. You know you could not put your bare finger in the socket of an electric fixture without a shock. Likewise I trust that as the Fires of the Kundalini are unlocked, you will guard well your attunement, your Harmony, and your connection with your Holy Christ Presence.

Ofttimes the awakening of this Fire is painful and causes great discomfort as it forges its way to new horizons. But if you will endure and allow the pathways to be opened, you will find waiting in the Secret Chamber of your Heart this pure Mother Light, ready to move into action and to become the many hands and feet of your lifestream.

Fire can be intimidating, and many who have for the first time seen the Inner Fires with their third-eye vision have pulled back. It takes Courage, beloved ones, to step into that intensity of Living Flame. Because you know that once you step into that Flame, the not-self of human creation, of all you think you are but are not, will be dissolved, and you will stand as the newborn babe before your very own God Presence, unclothed save for your own externalized Light.

> It takes Courage, beloved ones, to step into that intensity of Living Flame.

Many who count themselves our students consider they are not yet ready to take that step. For fear of loss they have chosen to stay in their former state. Such a waste of opportunity, beloved ones! Such tragic error! For there is no loss upon entering into the Fullness of the Flame of God. The Fullness of Love, of Light, of Compassion, of all the God Qualities you could ever desire are waiting for that moment when you courageously enter into the Fullness of the Flame.

Yes, the Fire may singe. Yes, it may be uncomfortable. Yes, the impersonal and personal opposition will try to disturb your world to keep you from entering into the

Fullness of the Flame. For it knows that once you have become the God Being of your own Reality — that Mighty I AM Presence — it no longer stands a chance of siphoning part of the daily allotment of your lifestream's Light. For instead you will be protected, clad in the Armor of Flame.

So what if all manner of chaos breaks loose just as you would step into that Flame. Recognize it for what it is, beloved ones. With single-mindedness of purpose, step forward into the Blazing Light of the Christ.

Those Saints of old, who are now Ascended, have gone before you and have left the record of their own overcoming, of the transitory pain and suffering of letting go of the unrealities of the human self in exchange for this Supernal Fire of Freedom. *There is no greater Joy than the Bliss of standing in the Fires of the Light of God and feeling the dross and the layers, the old karmic records falling off, never to appear again on the screen of life. For they are no more!*

**The greatest gift to mankind in this century has been the outer knowledge of the Violet Flame.**

Without question the greatest gift to mankind in this century has been the outer knowledge of the Violet Flame. For with this Flame you may consume all those records, you may consume the daily allotment of karma, so mitigated by your Holy Christ Presence.

Beloved ones, do you realize what this means? You no longer have to physically outpicture the pain and the anguish and the personal involvement of karmic ties simply for the sake of balancing the karma. All you need do is invoke the Flame, and by the Love of your I AM Presence, you will be flooded with Violet Fire coursing throughout your world.

Greet the day running with the Violet Flame as you receive your morning allotment of returning karma. Then after the Fire has burned through and transmuted all of the records, you will feel all sense of weight and burden lifted from your shoulders and be able to walk through your day with a lightness and an ability to breathe deeply.

Do you think, beloved ones, that We, Ascended Masters, were impervious to the karma and weight of the physical plane when We walked among you? We were not! We know every step of the Path you walk. We know what to expect. We know that as you turn the next corner you will have new challenges to meet. Our Desire is the God Desire to help you meet those challenges.

As you take the next step, visualize that step moving forward and creating a veritable pathway of Flame beneath your feet, and everywhere you walk you will leave blazing footprints for others to follow. Your example of overcoming will be as a talisman for the Light Bearers around you and those coming after.

*Recognize that you, yes you, beloved ones, are anchoring a Fire in the Earth that will raise the consciousness of mankind and allow for the Ascension of many to come.*

INVOKE THE FLAME! Even if you cannot see the Flames with your third-eye vision, you certainly can feel the warmth and intensity of their Radiation. Rest assured, beloved ones, the Fire will become quite tangible as you progress in its use! There is nothing hypothetical about the Sacred Fire surging through your world. And by your world, I don't just mean your physical body. I mean your affairs, your surroundings, your home, your workplace, your car, as well as your karma.

You have a magnificent tool, beloved ones, that for the most part goes unused. It is the gift of the throat chakra. The Blue Fire that emanates from the throat chakra is the Will of God bringing into outer manifestation the fulfillment of your calls. The forthright use of the power chakra coupled with Ascended Master Decrees, Fiats, and Affirmations will ignite the Fires of your Heart and draw down from the Ascended Master Octaves and Retreats of the Brotherhood the Fires anchored on our Altars. All you need to do is call. INVOKE THE FLAME!

Beloved ones, tend well the Immortal Victorious Threefold Flame ablaze now upon the Altar of your Heart. It is entrusted by your Presence into your keeping to protect, expand, and share that Flame when so guided with other lifestreams who are ready to receive the Flame of the Holy Spirit through you. Be not timid to speak of the Fire, for you will find that the more you speak of the Fires of the Will of God surging through your being, the more you will be illumined with the teaching to accompany that Will and the Compassion of the Heart to love life free in the Flame. The more you speak of the Fires of the Heart, the greater your Heart will burn, the closer your Presence will interact with you on a continual basis.

> *At long last you will be a walking, talking Son or Daughter of God bearing the message of Freedom and the Light for a planet so hungry, so thirsty that it cries out for fear that one of the Sons or Daughters of God will not look its way.*

You will look dispassionately upon the world as a child who misbehaves for attention and discipline from the parent and with the compassion of the Heart of Love of the Violet Flame.

Beloved ones, even the darkness and its denizens would rather be consumed by Violet Flame and repolarized back to the Heart of God than to continue on a path of death and destruction. Do you realize what I have just said? They cry aloud not for destruction, beloved ones, but for the liberation that you and you alone can offer.

*You are a Son or Daughter of God, capable of wielding Fire!* It is your Responsibility so to do. The astral plane

FIRE

> The calls you make, released by the Flame in your Heart, can change a world!

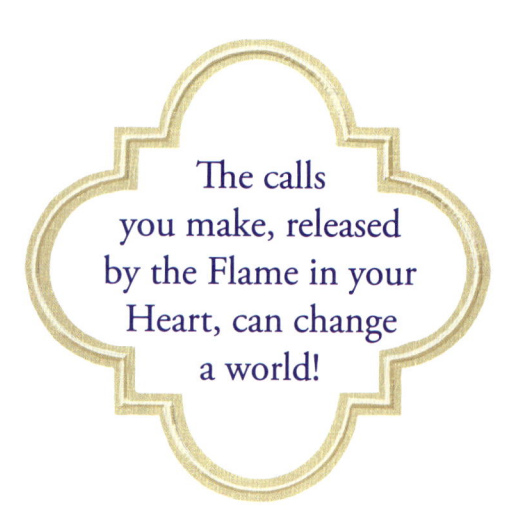

awaits deliverance. Will you not make the call and send the Light of God into action? Call forth the millions of Angels waiting, ready to move forward. The calls you make, released by the Flame in your Heart, can change a world, and not just this world, beloved ones, but other worlds! For you have a greater mission than just this world.

It is time for the Light Bearers to be up and doing. Do not shrink back from committing your life and yourself to this Cause for fear of loss of your own pseudo identity. Boldly wear the Mantle of your own Individualized God Presence. That is who you really are! Then move forward with the Legions of Light in the Fullness of the God Flame and you will be Victorious!

Be sealed in the Flame of your own God Presence in this hour of my *Visitation*. Feel the Fullness of that Flame surging through your being as a tangible reality. And then I, the Maha Chohan, will have the ability to direct my Flame of the Holy Spirit through you at any hour of the day or night.

### FIRE

I AM the Flame of God abiding throughout the body of Man!

## The Maha Chohan

*Beloved Mighty I AM Presence!*
*Charge and fill my feeling world*
*With your Great Ascended Master Fire!*

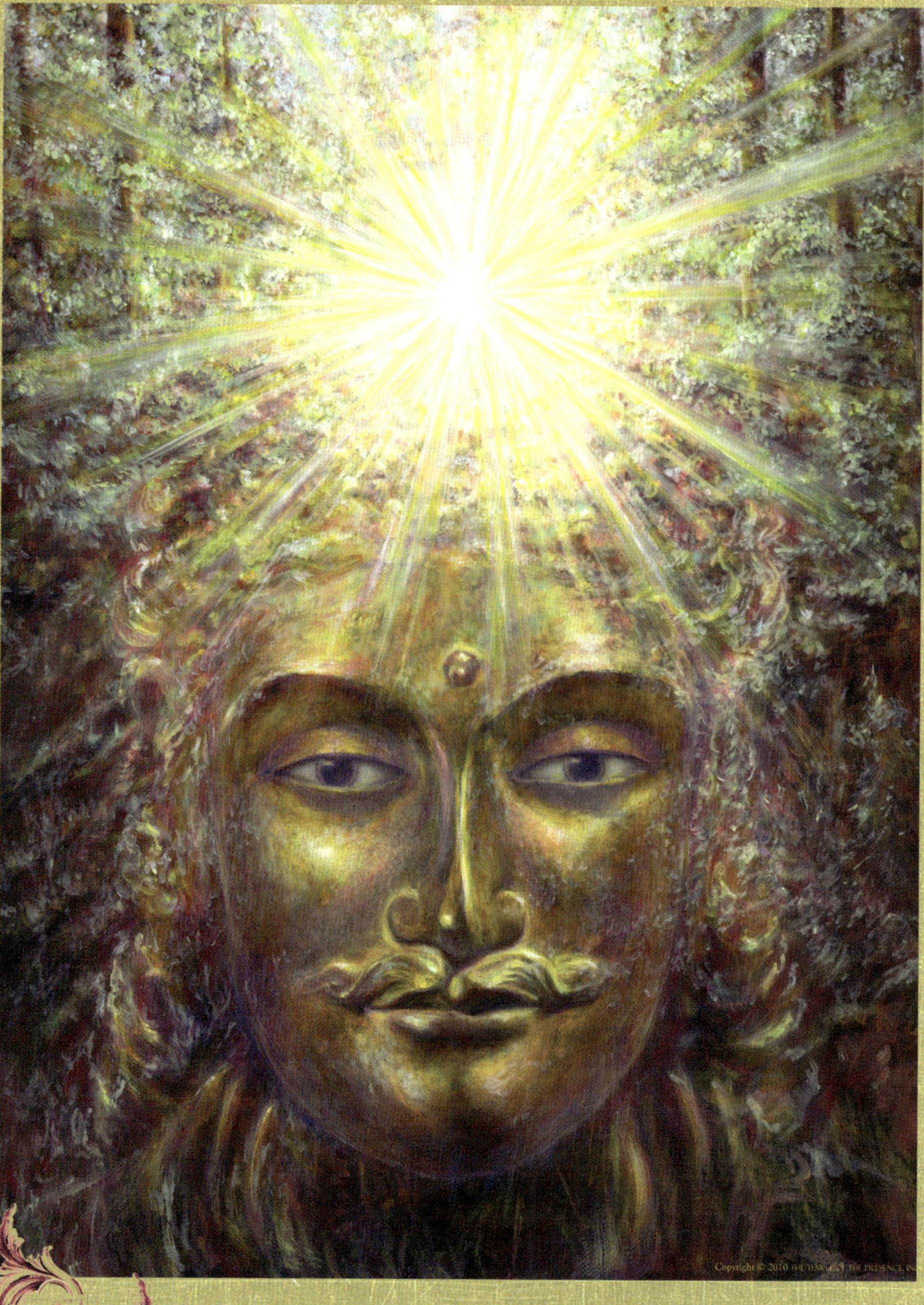
Copyright © 2010

# An Initiation in the Fire of the Ruby Chalice
## by Lord Maitreya

**H**AIL! Fiery Sons and Daughters of the Most High!

I AM Maitreya, Cosmic Christ and Planetary Buddha. I AM known as the Great Initiator, and I stand before you in this hour to bestow upon you a very scientific acceleration of Light. But first a word of caution. If this moment be not for you the hour of the *Visitation*, if you have not approached this *Ruby Chalice* with clean hands and heart, with complete and utter concentration and devotion to this ritual — the Sacred Ritual of drinking in our Presence — better to abide until that time when you can give your full measure of devotion. For this is indeed a Sacred Consecrated Hour when We stand in your aura precisely to pour into your world the unspeakably magnificent Supernal Light of our Ascended Presence.

Run to the altar! Love the Lord thy God with all thy Heart, with all thy soul, with all thy might. Pour forth the utmost devotion, the secret unspoken Adoration that has for so long remained locked and frozen upon the doorway of your Heart.

## Initiation

Having obeyed then the Great Command, I, Maitreya, stand before you, stretch forth the Wand of Fire, and circumscribe your Heart. I seal that precious Heart within the unbroken Circle of Sacred Fire that you might leap to your feet with the words of the prophet Isaiah on your lips, "Thou shalt not hurt nor destroy in all my Holy Mountain sayeth the Lord." Mark well this response of the Lord's Anointed when He too rejoiced at the transfiguring touch of God Love and sang this psalm of old.

Aflame with Adoration and Divine Love, I come with such surcease and succor to your Hearts as shall free you and ignite the kindling Christic Fire within you. This is the long forgotten Light of those transcendent Realms wherein your Blessed Holy Christ Presence abides. My brothers and my sisters, be not deceived by the dance of maya playing before your eyes.

Do not be so foolish as to weigh your own worth in God's Eyes by the irreverent witness, the coarseness, the hardness of heart, and the jostling of the world's restless energies upon your own. Surely you must be aware of the ongoing drama, the great work of salvation worked by myself and by my peers in Heaven. Surely you can have some of the awareness of the exertion on your behalf that goes on unceasingly at Inner Levels.

*It is all for Love of God in you!* We see what you do not! We value beyond all worldly treasures the Flame of God, endeavoring to burst through the chrysalis of the

Permanent Atom of your Heart. We strive and labor without ceasing for Love of you, knowing you as that Divine Presence seeking to be reborn here below.

Viewed from our level, We indeed see what you do not, of your true worth even in your present state. We care, and We are drawn always and ever to the musical Tone of your God Presence sounding through the night, sleeping ofttimes within the Spark of that Flame turned inwards in retreat from the harshness and the buffeting of the world and its ways. And so I come to initiate within that slumbering Spark of the Threefold Flame the intense frequency of Light which is the Fire of your own God Presence.

I speak to that Heart with the full Authority of my Office and I say, "Awake! Awake! Awake thou that sleepest! Now is the hour of your new birth!" Behold, a Star is born in the Firmament of Heaven. That which was in chrysalis, that which was as nebulae is ignited as Nova! All of the Cosmos witnesses the birth of a new Star! And the ritual of the Bethlehem Experience is multiplied throughout the land as was intended from the beginning.

Now my precious children you walk the Earth by the Light of your own Star! I have this day rekindled that Fire. I have breathed upon it the *Breath of Life,* and the smoldering coal which has been banked and slumbering for long ages leaps up and burns of its own Self-Luminous Fire! Do not search the world or its confines for this Light. By that I mean to include all of the matter planes.

Such transcendent Fire cannot be contained within such paltry vessels. They can only absorb a minor portion of its Radiation, a secondary allotment if you will. For this Christ Light — this Cosmic Christ Light native to your own Christ Identity — abides in cosmic dimensions where time and space are not.

Let your Heart roam free then throughout the untrammeled Realms which have always been its Home, and along the way it will share the fullest measure possible with the lower worlds of earth, air, fire, and water. But the cup of your outer vessels must await the midnight hour of Transfiguration, the dawn of Resurrection, and the glorious noontide Reality of the Ascension before they too shall taste of this Freedom in its Fullness.

Precious ones, be not confused. Do not make the mistake of analyzing this Initiation with the outer mind or seeking to compartmentalize this Fire with the intellect. For in so doing you would compress that Light back into the Secret Chamber of the Heart, once again barely releasing its Fire. Understand only that this Flame is the Heart of the God Being whom you are in its Fullness in higher dimensions and in Cosmic Space where North, South, East, and West mean far more than you can possibly imagine.

This Heart then is where you and your I AM Presence are one. Let it suffice for you to liberate that Heart to do what Hearts naturally do, which is to radiate Fire, to shine as a Sun, to glow with the effulgent Fires that are the *Sun-behind-the-Sun.* If you will let your Heart roam free, then I will have succeeded in giving you a taste of what it means to stand above the waters of this world and be free.

I remind you of the words of the Christos in the hours of his final Initiations as He sought in his most poignant manner to demonstrate once and for all eternity the cosmic worth of each Divine Ray of the Monad. "The servant is not greater than his Lord." Saying thus, He bathed the feet of the disciples in honor of their Mighty I AM Presence, the Great God Being whom He beheld striving to express through the weights and veils of the flesh.

And so inasmuch as that Holy One whom I know so well at Inner Levels who is your God Self has deemed fit to descend into these matter planes and abides here below unto this very hour, therefore do I direct the Cherubim of Adoration to tarry before the Altar of your Starfire Christic Heart Flame. Lawfully do they adore, love, and worship that Flame, for where it burns, there is the Altar of the Most High, the Altar of the One True and Living God.

If you will suffer these Cherubim an eternal place of Sanctity and Holiness within this Electronic Circle of Fire which I have inscribed about you, then in those hours when your attention is required elsewhere, by *their* Love and attention on your Heart Flame, these Cherubim will sustain that Effulgent Radiance through your flesh form. For the God Flame can abide only where it is constantly giving and receiving that Fohat of Love which is its Divine Nature.

If you would be wise, if you truly mean what you affirm with your lips, if you hunger and thirst after Righteousness, you will tend this Fire daily and by your Adoration poured forth to the Mighty God Presence dwelling within you, this Flame will increase and you shall move through your everyday life bathed in this ever expanding Radiance of Sacred Fire poured into space.

Beloved ones, I trust that you will accept my rhapsody on your Heart, your own Christ Flame. Poets, balladeers, and musicians are sometimes better capable of drawing forth and expressing those subtle and yet splendid frequencies of the Higher Octaves. Today I have sought to interpret one of these Divine Attributes that you might see and behold with true Vision. Enter into this God Vision and live this God Life which is our constant Joy!

In closing, may I remind you once again of the stirring admonition of your Sponsor and Friend, El Morya,

*Elevate the Chalice!*

*It shall be filled!*

*Drink ye all of It!*

*Lord Maitreya*

INITIATION

170